# Journey to Joy

Luang Phaw Dhammajayo

Copyrighted by
Tawandhamma Foundation
P.O. Box 122
Khlong Luang District
Pathumthani Province
Thailand 12120
info@tawandhamma.org
www.tawandhamma.org

Published by
Foundation of Wisdom Perfection
Mr. Somchai Laopeamthong
88/136 Mu 4, Charoensuk 4 Village
Soi Senanikom 1, Paholyotin Road
Chorakaebua Sub-District
Ladprao District, Bangkok
Thailand 10230
Tel: (66+2) 553-0496, (66+8) 1494-9072

Edited, Designed, and Distributed by
The Print Lodge Pte Ltd
16 Arumugam Road
#03-04 Lion Building D
Singapore 409961
info@theprintlodge.com.sg
Tel: (65) 6746 6520



ISBN: 978-981-05-9637-8 (Singapore)

Printed in Thailand by Rung Silp Printing

# Contents

# *Introduction*

Life is a journey, a journey heading toward the desired destination of happiness and success involving our family, our studies, our career, and other goals, both material and spiritual. The journey of life for everyone occurs everywhere and everyday whether we are aware of it or not. When we mention the word 'journey', we often have the common stereotype of an external journey. This makes us unable to discover true happiness in life.

The external journey refers to the movement from one point to another point, no matter in which direction or by which vehicle. In order to reach our destination, we may journey with our own effort by passing through danger, wasting money, and sometimes losing our wealth, physical organs or even our lives. An external journey creates tedium, temporary joy and limited experiences. As time flies by, we feel bored and forget the joy we had.

There is another kind of journey known to only a few, which is the internal journey by way of meditation. This is quite different from the external journey because one takes no risks or faces any danger. It is the journey through joyfulness and revival. When we meditate correctly, our bodies and minds will be relaxed. The whole world becomes a pleasure for us. All of this starts from having stillness of the mind with our eyes closed, in a peaceful position known as the meditation posture. Then, we will be able to taste a genuine sense of peace.

We will experience infinite happiness which will continuously add up.

Nothing surpasses the bliss from meditation. There is no need for physical, verbal or mental force. This kind of happiness does not exist in the external world. It is more profound and permanent. We will understand much better when we practise and attain our meditation goals by ourselves. Besides, happiness from meditation can also help to develop and improve our quality of life and the quality of the entire world.

This book is a manual for one's life journey and speaks of the principles and methods of an internal journey through meditation until reaching one's destination or the attainment of Dhammakaya, the true refuge within everyone.

This is the true journey of every life, the path that brings happiness and success in all aspects. There are also personal stories of various meditators throughout the world who have started their internal journeys and are willing to share their experience with the hope that you will be among those who join this journey in achieving immortal happiness.

# *The Beginning of Life's Journey*

*Even having travelled for a long time,*
*By land, sky, and ocean,*
*Reaching as far as the stars,*
*You have not really journeyed at all.*
*Life does not begin with the body,*
*Nor the journey measured with time*
*Or distance travelled,*
*As one may misunderstand.*
*It begins the day you close your eyes,*
*Relaxed in both body and mind,*
*Visualising the shining sun within.*
*That is the true beginning of life's journey,*
*Whose end is the ultimate destination,*
*Of abounding eternal happiness.*

Luang Phaw Dhammajayo

*28 March 2006*

# PART 1

# The Beginning of the Journey

*Chapter 1*

# The Universality of Meditation

"To not think at all, anyone of any religion in this world can do, whether one is a Buddhist, Christian, Muslim, Hindu and so on. To not do something is not against the law, is not immoral and does not go against any ancient tradition. It does not go against the beliefs of any religion. Simply close your eyes and do nothing."

**Luang Phaw Dhammajayo**

## Transcending All Differences

Meditation is a universal act that everyone in this world can do. All can practise it regardless of nationality, religion, or ethnicity. All one needs is a human body. The air is a universal element in this world, in which everyone can breathe. No matter where we go in the planet, we will find air. Meditation is like the air – universal and essential.



If we do not close our minds, but rather, consider it carefully, we realise that we can still follow the religion we believe in and incorporate meditation. To not think at all, anyone of any religion in this world can do, whether one is a Buddhist, Christian, Muslim, Hindu, and so on. To not do something is not against the law, is not immoral, and does not go against any ancient tradition. Simply close your eyes and do nothing. In other words, meditate. It is a practice that will bring our lives happiness and fulfillment, which we should take utmost care to preserve.

## *Searching for the Truth*

In the Pali language, ***'natthi santiparaṃ sukhaṃ' means 'there is no happiness other than the peace of mind.'*** **The happiness that one cannot explain with words is the happiness that arises from a still mind in meditation.** The attainment of inner happiness is something that everyone can do if we give ourselves the opportunity. Does truth exist? Does true happiness exist? We can discover the answers to these questions and then share them with the world.

The first step is to search for the truth. Meditate and clarify the mind. When we do so, happiness will be within reach. It is like when we are about to learn a foreign language. We must forget our native language to learn the new. Study the subject of life in the same manner. You must forget other things temporarily. Then you will discover the many benefits of meditation.



This knowledge is the universal knowledge that everyone has the right to learn. We must seek the answers within ourselves, by ourselves. We will be both the student and the teacher. The library of true knowledge is within us. It can be accessed by closing your eyes and expanding the mind. If you search for the answer, you will find it.

Therefore, if people in the world temporarily forget their differences in religion, personal beliefs, traditions, customs, or cultures, and allow their minds to open, they can begin practising meditation and reaching true inner happiness. There are many religious followers who have opened their minds to the practice of meditation. Their perception of the world evolved from one of suffering to indescribable happiness. More and more people, adults and children, are beginning to experience this as they open their minds and follow the right principles.

## *Different Shells but the Same Core*

Differences arise as we grow up and start to recognise the variation in nationality, religion, race, skin colour, social status, appearance, etc. Differences can contribute to division and conflict. But once we close our eyes, the differences disappear. Thus, we should close our eyes to seek the universal happiness inside. When we see the universal truth, all differences will become insignificant. The conflicts in this world will vanish. We will think, speak, and act in harmony. In other words, we will think only about virtuous deeds, resulting in the progression of good Dhamma. Goodwill and fellowship will arise. People will seek happiness from giving, not just by taking or receiving. It will be as if there are no borders. We will all feel a sense of belonging to the same brotherhood.



## *The Universal Sentiment Expressed*

People may have external differences, but their innermost self is the same. It is the similarities that transcend their differences.

Nationality or religion does not matter. After they bring their minds to a standstill, all of them describe the same feeling: that meditation brings about great unlimited happiness that they have never encountered before.

If everyone in the world has the same goal or dream of seeing true peace in the world, a world with no borders, no soldiers, no police, a world where people have only love and good wishes for each other, true peace will not be difficult to achieve. **True world peace begins with inner peace, when our minds are still and calm.** Once everyone can do this, true world peace can happen at this very moment.

To share in the same dream, we must learn and experience meditation altogether. However, people cannot communicate effectively with one another yet. There are many barriers in our communication, such as custom, tradition, culture, language and geography. If we can overcome these barriers and communicate to the world about how to still the mind, we will have true world peace. This is not just a dream, but a determination to make it a reality.

# *Chapter 2*

# An Ancient Secret for the New Millennium

"The Dhammakaya is the pure and original nature residing in every human being regardless of their nationality, religion, or ethnicity. We can call this the pure original state or whatever we choose, but Buddhist scholars call it the Dhammakaya. In simple terms, where there are human beings, there is the Dhammakaya."

**Luang Phaw Dhammajayo**

## *True Happiness along the Middle Way*

Every person in the world desires happiness, hates suffering, and hopes to find true fulfillment. But billions of people have yet to learn the nature of true happiness. What is it and how can it be achieved?

These were the circumstances before the birth of the Lord Buddha more than 2,500 years ago: The Lord Buddha gave his life over to experimentation in the science of the mind until he discovered the practice of meditation along the Middle Way. When he followed the Middle Way, he found inner peace, wisdom and true happiness. The meditation he taught is a universal method that people of all nationalities and religions are able to practise even though their faiths may differ from one another.

The true happiness sought by all people can be found within each of us. It is not an external power or object. The method for reaching this happiness is to completely still the mind. When the mind reaches a state of complete stillness, happiness will follow swiftly. Nothing else is necessary. However, if stillness cannot be accomplished, true happiness will remain unattainable. Make the mind centred and calm during every activity: while sitting, standing, walking or sleeping. An indescribable happiness will overflow from within.

# *LUANG PU WAT PAKNAM and the Return of the Dhammakaya*

The Great Masters of meditation have told us that the knowledge of meditation practice along the Middle Way was lost 500 years after the Lord Buddha passed away into *Nibbana* (Nirvana).



It was rediscovered in 1916 by the Great Master Phramongkolthepmuni (Luang Pu Wat Paknam), a very determined Buddhist monk, as he sat in the main chapel at Wat Boad Bon in Bangkuvieng Sub-district, Nonthaburi Province, Thailand, on the full moon day of the tenth lunar month. At that time, he was 33 years old and had spent 11 years as an ordained monk.

He made a whole-hearted resolution to himself that day, that unless he attained enlightenment as the Lord Buddha had done, he would not rise for any reason from meditation, even if it meant his death. Persevering, he sat in meditation the entire night and found the Middle Way and reached the Body of Enlightenment residing in him, which is called the *Dhammakaya.*



The *Dhammakaya* is the pure and original nature residing in every human being regardless of their nationality, religion, or ethnicity. We can call this the pure original state or whatever we choose but Buddhist scholars call it the *Dhammakaya.* In simple terms, where there are human beings, there is the *Dhammakaya.*

The word *Dhammakaya* is from the Pali language, a language used to record Buddhist scriptures. It means "The Body of Enlightenment" or "The Body of Truth". It is an ancient word which appears in various versions of Buddhist scriptures used by various Buddhist traditions, including the *Theravada, Mahayana*, and *Vajrayana*. It has spread into a variety of languages all over the world. In other words, it is not a new concept, but rather, it is an ancient one from the time of the Lord Buddha.



During the time that its knowledge was lost, people who had heard of the word *Dhammakaya* did not understand what it was, and they could not find an explanation of the practice that would help lead them to attain the *Dhammakaya*. This was the case until Luang Pu Wat Paknam offered his own existence to the Lord Buddha and re-discovered the *Vijja Dhammakaya* (the Wisdom of Dhammakaya Meditation) of the Lord Buddha. This made the word *Dhammakaya*, in the Buddhist scriptures, return to life again. This is an inheritance for the world which the Great Master bestowed to all people. Its knowledge gives us confidence in our meditation and enables us to attain true happiness while living on earth. When we attain the *Dhammakaya*, we will know ourselves and our true nature.



**The *Dhammakaya* is the primary source of true happiness, pure wisdom and infinite compassion. Everyone can attain the *Dhammakaya* by making their minds completely still. Keep the mind centred in the body. Once you achieve the *Dhammakaya*, you will feel a wonderful sense of comfort and security along with a feeling of confidence and self-reliance.**

You can be alone without feeling lonely. Sadness is only in the past; wellbeing and joy are your constant companions. Upon attaining the *Dhammakaya*, ignorance transforms to understanding, indifference to awareness. Your minds will expand to encompass pure and essential knowledge. And a sense of fellowship for all humankind will grow.



## *To Stop at the Seventh Base of the Mind*

Luang Pu Wat Paknam devoted himself to meditation all his life. From the time he ordained as a monk until his last day on earth, he meditated diligently every day without fail. **Through his singular determination, he found the seventh base of the mind, which**

**is two finger-widths above the navel level. This is the true resting place of the mind and the starting point of the journey along the Middle Way.**

In this spot, the mind is at a completely neutral point, a private world unto itself. It is a tranquil corner where we are free from thoughts, worries, and fears. Here can be found the wellspring of purity that invigorates us to perform good deeds without fear or anxiety.



Moreover, **Luang Pu Wat Paknam was able to explain the method of meditation for attaining the *Dhammakaya*: "To stop is to succeed". This is done by leading the mind to rest, easily and comfortably at the seventh base of the mind.** If the mind is still, it becomes clear and refined. We will reach the truth in ourselves.

Therefore, to stop and still the mind is to succeed. We should lead our minds to the centre of our bodies as often as possible, even as we perform our daily routine. With continual practice, our minds will become increasingly still and we will arrive at the limitless peace and serenity of the *Dhammakaya*.



Throughout Luang Pu Wat Paknam's life, he taught the *Dhammakaya* Meditation at Wat Paknam Bhasicharoen (Paknam Temple in Bhasicharoen district). He sent his disciples, both monks and nuns, to disseminate the teachings in many places. This brought wide acceptance of *Dhammakaya* Meditation, both in Thailand and abroad. **Among his numerous students was a Buddhist nun who meditated so well that the Great Master praised her, saying, "Chand is second to none". He was referring**

**to the distinguished meditation teacher, the Master Nun Chand Khonnokyoong (Khun Yay Ajahn), who later founded Wat Phra Dhammakaya.**

## *From a Barren Field*



I was not born in time to study with the Great Master. I mainly learned about *Dhammakaya* Meditation from Khun Yay Ajahn. I obtained some knowledge from monastic teachers who were her contemporaries, but my principle understanding came from Khun Yay Ajahn herself. From her, I felt a great sense of love and harmony. She was kind to me. I sat in meditation with her continuously, from the time I was a student at the university and went for meditation together with my school friends at Wat Paknam Bhasicharoen. When we graduated, some of us ordained as monks and others became lay volunteers. This was the community that pioneered the construction of Wat Phra Dhammakaya. At that time, Khun Yay Ajahn was 60 years old, but she devoted all her energy to the temple's construction. At that time, the temple grounds were only open fields.

**Wat Phra Dhammakaya commenced with meditation because the *Dhammakaya* resides in every human being. Whatever your nationality or religion, whether you are educated or not, you have the *Dhammakaya.* Wherever human beings are located, the *Dhammakaya* exists. Wat Phra Dhammakaya was constructed to preserve and nurture this spirit.** Initially the temple brought the community together to meditate. Later it gained popularity because people with wisdom wanted to test the *Dhammakaya*'s existence and came to meditate. The desire for knowledge of the *Dhammakaya* Meditation grew and the number of people coming to the temple expanded. Meditation first took place under trees, then later under tents. When the numbers expanded beyond the tents' capacity, it was necessary to construct the Catummaharajika Pavilion which could seat 500 people. It was thought that this was all that was needed. It was possible to sit in meditation and teach one subject: how to attain the *Dhammakaya*.



More people continued to come to the temple so that a pavilion meant for 500 people had to accommodate 5,000. The temple had to rent hundreds of tents and the financial burden became excessive. So, the straw-roofed Meditation Hall was built. It could seat more than 10,000 people, and we thought it to be adequate since no other place had 10,000 people sitting in meditation together. But soon 30,000 people came, so it became necessary to rent tents as before. With the original straw-roofed Meditation Hall unable to accommodate the growing community, we began construction on the World Dhammakaya Centre. The Centre is composed of more than 320 hectares of land. It was believed that this would be enough to welcome people from all over the world who are interested in learning to meditate and in finding true happiness. We have welcomed guests from all nationalities, languages and religions to practise and teach meditation at the Centre.



In 2002, The Inner Dreams Kindergarten Programme was established to share knowledge with all students, knowledge from the Tripitaka (the Buddhist Scriptures), from Khun Yay Ajahn, and most importantly, from the *Dhammakaya*

Meditation and also to express gratitude to all those who offer food and necessities to the monastic community. These offerings to the monks and novices provide us with the mental and physical energy for studying Dhamma and maintaining the code of monastic discipline bequeathed by the Lord Buddha.



The Inner Dreams Kindergarten Programme is based on making learning enjoyable. In the early days of the School, students joined the school via telephone. They would pick up the telephone and take delight in listening to stories about the true nature of life. Later, the School spread to the Internet (www.dmc.tv/en). Presently, the School broadcasts globally via satellite television.

Students attend a single class, which is composed of men and women of all ages and religious beliefs, where they watch, meditate, and learn about the Dhamma. Together they accumulate great merit. Through what they learned, some students' lives underwent great transformation, others gradually made adjustments. Hearing about these positive changes, other students, who are less diligent about meditating, become more dedicated. Each student's success encourages the others. This is what invigorates me and gives me the energy to continue teaching.

**I dream that all families and all households around the world will meditate together via satellite broadcasts. Together we will attain true inner happiness, see the brightness inside,**

**and enter the Body of Truth within us: the *Dhammakaya*.** This has been a dream of mine for a long time. I have relied on satellite broadcasts to share the meditation experiences of the students in the Inner Dreams Kindergarten Programme to people across the globe. These students, who come from such diverse backgrounds, unite to meditate and perform deeds of universal goodness.

# PART 2

# Open your Heart to the Journey

# Chapter 3

# Love and Family

"Spouses should cherish each other. The longer they live together, the more they should care for one another. By caring for each other, they remain youthful and content; therefore, we should allow goodness to nourish mutual compassion for one another. If there is a quarrel, the couple should act as lions do. When two lions confront each other, one will crouch down and end the quarrel peacefully. This acquiescence is not a loss; instead it is a victory of the mind, preventing the couple from becoming slaves to mutual rage. Love and compassion should be reciprocated; anger should not be answered by anger, but by calmness. Then, the couple will be able to maintain healthy married lives."

**Luang Phaw Dhammajayo**

## *Love in the Right Way*

From the first moment of life to the last, humans have a natural need for love. We feel satisfied when we are loved, and we are miserable when we do not receive love. If we are never loved or if we never love anyone, life seems barren and hollow, as if it lacks some vital energy required to progress with confidence or success. Nevertheless, when people have a bad experience in love, they may reject it completely, afraid of loving again until they do not know how to love anymore. Actually, despite bad experiences, everyone is capable of learning to love wisely. The right love will bestow happiness and also allow us to be reborn as human beings.

If we want someone to love us, we have to make ourselves lovable. There are four ways to do so. First, we have to learn to give, whether it is love, a smile, compassion, material things, or knowledge. Second, we have to speak kindly. Third, we have to be helpful and considerate. If we can help other people in any way through our actions, influence, and intelligence, we should do so. When we encourage others to succeed, we will receive love. Lastly, we have to always conduct ourselves appropriately no matter what our status is, whether we are parents, children, employers, subordinates or even friends.



## The True Goal of Marriage

Our love is not only given to parents, siblings, and friends, but also shared with someone who may become one's husband or wife. If we understand the true goal of marriage, we can build a healthier relationship, and in turn spread positive energy to those around us even beyond the marriage.

Some may decide to marry based on physical appearances only. This decision seems short-sighted. Since youth and beauty fade over time and burdens increase with age, a couple's feelings will fade away too. Dissatisfaction will grow and conflicts may arise more frequently until they become irreconcilable family problems.



**On the other hand, if we enter into marriage hoping to find an intimate friend with whom we can build good deeds and together reach the goal of human rebirth, the expectations and results will be different. No matter how young or how old we are, each will grow, cherish, persuade, and encourage the other to do good deeds until the day we die.**

To this purpose, marriage is not based solely on whether we feel physical attraction for the person, but more importantly, whether this person has similar faith, views, and beliefs. It takes a long time to learn about all of these qualities in another person.

## *Anger at Different Times, but Love at the Same Time*



Selecting a spouse is a life-changing decision. Out of the billions of people on earth, we choose only one with whom to spend the rest of our lives with. But choosing is not the most difficult part. It is living together afterwards, and building a healthy marriage, that is the most challenging.

In order to create a warm and loving family, it is necessary for spouses to speak with each other kindly. This means using polite, respectful, truthful and constructive words. Kind words make love sweeter. Warmth and a sense of security will pervade the household. Spouses should cherish each other. The longer they live together, the more they should care for each other. By caring for each other, they remain youthful and content; therefore, we should allow goodness to nourish mutual compassion for one another. If there is a quarrel, the couple should act as lions do. When two lions confront each other, one will crouch down and end the quarrel peacefully. This acquiescence is not a loss; instead it is a victory of the mind, preventing the couple from becoming slaves to mutual rage. Love and compassion should be reciprocated; anger should not be answered by anger, but by calmness. Then, the couple will be able to maintain healthy married lives.

A family is a small but vital unit in society. In addition to building a strong and healthy marriage, a couple who plan to become parents must learn how to love children. Parents should be knowledgeable about the best direction to take when encouraging their children. They should teach them to do good deeds instead of allowing a babysitter or a television to raise them. To be good role models for their children, parents should learn and practise doing good deeds themselves.

## *Loving Ourselves*

When we talk about loving ourselves, we are not referring to selfishness. Learning to love ourselves is very important. **If we love ourselves correctly, we will reach true happiness. In fact, out of correct love of the self will bloom**

**universal love, the love of all of humankind without expectation of reward or gain.**

To love ourselves in the appropriate way, we have to still the mind by relaxing and gently closing our eyes, bringing the mind to the centre of our bodies. When the mind comes to a standstill, it will fall down as if into an air pocket. Then, a light much like sunlight will shine brightly inside of your mind, glowing as if we have cleansed our bodies, speech and minds of contamination. By practising meditation in this way, you will learn to create peace and serenity in your lives. Blossoming from the positive emotions created, which feels unlike anything we have previously experienced, we will soon learn to love ourselves. We have been looking for this happiness, but could never find it. Through meditation, we will achieve a level of self-love and self-reliance that we never thought we could feel. When we depend on other people for comfort, there is always a chance of conflict or disappointment, but with a mind clarified through meditation, solitude becomes natural and you will never feel tension or anger. By closing our eyes lightly, relaxing and stilling the mind at the centre of our bodies, we progress toward the source of true love and happiness, which can be found deep within each of us.



## *Universal Love*

**Universal love is a love for everyone. There is no lust or desire involved. With goodwill we wish for everyone to find happiness in body and mind and to attain the *Dhammakaya*.** In order for us to discover universal love, we must see the world through the bright inner light of meditation, which will allow us to perceive the world as it truly is. Every living being will appear as its true self and we will realise that our lives and others' lives are equal and worthy. If we find ourselves more fortunate than others, we will feel compelled to assist them. This is the power of universal love.



When we come to know about *Dhammakaya*, and are united with the Body of Dhamma, we will want to spread the knowledge to all of humankind without expectation of anything in return. We will want to see all of humankind attain the Body of Dhamma as we have. This desire completely differs in scope and feeling from the desires we feel when we do not know the Body of Dhamma.

I would like to see everyone use these ideas and techniques to build happiness and understanding within your families. Try to follow the good examples of the Inner Dreams Kindergarten Programme students who have introduced this meditation technique to their family members. They have noticed a change in their home environments, with delight replacing anxiety and happiness transforming from grief. Let their example teach us.

Mr. Richard Braun (Germany)



"Meditation to attain the *Dhammakaya* has restrained me from having bad thoughts. When I have bad thoughts, I can clear them out very quickly before I end up feeling sorry about doing bad deeds or saying bad words. I have quit smoking, permanently. My wife and I are more at peace. We care for each other more deeply than before."

My name is Richard Braun. I am German and I have been married to a woman for 13 years. In the past, those who visited us could sense the heat in our home despite the very cold weather of Germany. This is because both my wife and myself were very temperamental. We never give in to each other. We usually fight and exchange harsh words. It was like throwing rocks at each other. I do not feel comfortable saying pleasant words such as, "I love my wife". I do not see the necessity of saying those words. The only time I said, "I love you", was the day I proposed to her 15 years ago. In addition, I had been smoking for 37 years.

My life changed when my wife received a Dhamma VCD from the monk at the Hanover Meditation Centre. While she watched the VCD, I could feel the power of Luang Phaw's voice in that VCD although I could not understand Thai. It was full of love and kindness. It inspired me to quit smoking for good and also inspired me to try meditation. Both my wife and I began meditating in order to attain the *Dhammakaya*.

Since I don't understand Thai, I received very little information regarding meditation using the *Dhammakaya* technique. I was told to place my mind inside my body, two inches above the navel level and allow it to remain there. I could use a clear crystal ball as an object of meditation. That's all I learned.

In the first five days of meditation, I could not see anything except darkness. But I could feel the serenity. On the sixth day, my mind came to a standstill. I first saw a small shining star inside my body. I tried to control my excitement. Later, the star enlarged and the crystal body of the *Dhammakaya* appeared inside. The *Dhammakaya* was as bright as the sun, but the sight brought me a cool feeling and it felt comfortable to my eyes. I could feel the happiness that radiated from the centre of my body. It was so great that I could not keep it to myself.



My wife was so astonished that a student like me could attain a better experience than her trainer. I think no one can explain the happiness that I received, and nothing in this world can compare.

That experience encouraged me to meditate more. I currently meditate about 2 or 5 hours a day. In the past, it took me some time to free all the thoughts from my mind. I would have to take a deep breath to do so. If it did not work, I would recite the mantra, "Samma Arahang". Now, I can let go of all my thoughts as soon as I sit down to meditate and close my eyes. I can see the body of the *Dhammakaya* inside me when I meditate, or even when I drive a car, or have my meal, or take a bath. Sometimes, I can see the *Dhammakaya* rising up from the centre of my body, one by one like pearls on a necklace, the new pearl emerging more beautifully than the previous one.



The largest *Dhammakaya* body that I ever saw was as big as the Zugspiter Mountain. It is the tallest mountain in Germany. The *Dhammakaya* body was brighter than sunlight and very beautiful. It was a wonderful feeling. My body was so light, it was as if it was going to disappear. My mind was so light and I felt so happy that I cannot explain the feeling I had in words.

I have tried meditating before, using many other techniques. But I feel that the *Dhammakaya* technique is best suited for me. I like the way that I don't have to do anything more to attain happiness. Presently, my wife and I do the chanting and meditate everyday after work. When I meditate, I listen to Luang Phaw Dhammajayo's teachings to comfort and calm my mind. I close my eyes, loosen my mind and clear all my thoughts.

Meditation to attain the *Dhammakaya* has restrained me from having bad thoughts. When I have bad thoughts, I can clear them out very quickly before I end up feeling sorry about doing bad deeds or saying bad words. I have quit smoking, permanently. My wife and I are more at peace. We care for each other more deeply than before. I tell her everyday that I love her. I choose my words with care when I talk to her. She says that I am no longer a husband who speaks harshly and I think she is no longer a wife who complains as much. She says that I am filled with love, but I think that is because she is lovely. In the end, we have transformed from being a temperamental couple to being a couple that people want to become acquainted with.

**Mr. Koichi Enomoto (Japan)**



“My daughter is a kid and likes to have fun just like other kids, yet she follows her mother to the Meditation Centre. She has improved on herself and I'm impressed. She loves and respects her mother and father very much. I feel that my wife is like a friend, a co-worker and an advisor to me. We have the same goal and I would like to walk along with her, hand in hand towards reaching that goal.”

My name is Koichi Enomoto. I am Japanese. As the only son, I was well looked after. I had no siblings to share and learn the intricacies of giving and taking with, thus I didn't know the virtue of giving. My parents were my givers, and they gave me more than I could give back to them. I had a great deal of freedom in my life, especially when I became a teenager. I had friends; we drank alcohol and smoked cigarettes. This was a traditional habit among Japanese teenagers. When I got a job, I did not slow down my habit of seeking fun, in fact, I spoiled myself even more and spent my salary each time I received it.



My family had no faith in any religion or any god. My father lived through World War II and most Japanese exhibited confident personalities during that time. Being his son, I was naturally influenced to be as confident as him.

Then, one day, marking a turning point in my life, I met the woman who evidently became my wife. As the days progressed, I discovered that she was kind and caring. I believed she acquired these qualities from Buddhism. She had never refused soliciting from anyone and she accumulated merit and meditated regularly. One day, she learnt of the Dhammakaya Meditation Centre in Tokyo. There were Buddhist monks from Thailand performing deeds of merit at the centre. When she returned home, she would advise me to do the same, but I didn't have that much faith in Buddhism yet, so I did not take this matter seriously. However, that did not prevent me from going to the Centre because I know Buddhism cultivated and refined her mind.

When Luang Phaw Dhammajayo planned to expand the Dhamma satellite network throughout the world, I had an opportunity to study Dhamma further. At the centre in Tokyo, there was a need to translate Dhamma into Japanese. A member of the staff at the Tokyo centre, who is now a monk, invited me to help translate Dhamma. In this way, I gradually learned to understand and know more about Dhamma. I learned generosity, the five precepts and meditation. I started to meditate little by little and I think that helped me to relax.



When I tried to practise meditation for the first time, it was not easy for me at all. At the beginning, I was aching and stiff. In addition, I felt very sleepy. Since I was not familiar with sitting on the floor, I felt pain in my legs. So, I changed my position and sat on a chair. Although this position helped me to withstand longer, I still didn't really understand the method and benefits of meditation. The staff at the Meditation Centre in Tokyo encouraged and introduced me to the possibility of relaxation in meditation. I also received a crystal ball from one of the monks who helped me. I held the crystal ball in my hand and practised meditation. I was able to visualise the crystal ball in my abdomen. My body felt so light and it seemed like my mind merged and became one with the crystal ball. Finally, I was able to sit in the standard position as taught by the Great Master Phramongkolthepmuni.

Sometimes, I thought that the crystal ball and the crystal body that I saw in my meditation were due to my own visualisation. But, indeed, I found that if I used my mind to think of the crystal ball or crystal body, my feelings would not be light and relaxed at all. So when I meditated, I simply generated a feeling as if there was a crystal ball in my abdomen. Soon, I would see it with my mind. Then, I would feel fresh, light, and soothed. It was a wonderful feeling that I have never experienced before. When I felt sleepy, I would recite the mantra "Samma Arahang". I imagined that the mantra emerged from the middle of the crystal ball. My mind would revolve around the mantra continuously until I would completely forget the sleepiness. I didn't even understand how my feeling of sleepiness left me. I only knew that the mantra "Samma Arahang" emerged from the centre of the crystal ball at the middle of my abdomen.



Japan is a country in which people work for long hours. Working Japanese men rarely have time to converse with their children because they have to leave their homes early in the morning and return late at night. For myself, I think meditation is necessary apart from working. On weekdays, I meditate for at least 30 to 60 minutes. On Sundays, I will meditate with Luang Phaw Dhammajayo during every session of the satellite broadcast on television. I think meditation is a must for modern Japanese society. Although Japanese are very advanced in technology, they have a high suicide rate. Since they have no spiritual refuge, they can't think of a good solution to sustain their own lives.



Working life in Japan is quite stressful. The company that I work for is a large and famous company, so employees have to work hard for the company. I cannot help but feel immense pressure from work. When I am stressed out from work, I bring this stress home with me. This, of course, contributes to an unpleasant atmosphere. Even though we never fight with each other, I can sense an uneasy feeling developing in our family. But after I practised meditation and got involved with activities at the meditation centre regularly, our family's relationship has improved and I have better control of my emotions.

In my company, I spearheaded a team named "Do-ray-me-fa" to plan, advise, improve work efficiency, ensure product quality and take care of the environment. I also managed an accident prevention team known as the "KY" team.

After meditating, I had always wished for troubles among my co-workers to disappear. Ever since then, I never had any troubles with anyone. Compared to how I was like in the past, I found that I could adjust myself very well at work. My work went well as planned and I was able to work well with others. There was no stress at all and relationships in our team improved greatly.

Even Kimie, my daughter who is a kid and likes to have fun just like other kids, follows her mother to the Meditation Centre. She has improved on herself and I'm impressed. She loves and respects her mother and father very much. I feel that my wife is like a friend, a co-worker, and an advisor to me. We have the same goal and I would like to walk along with her, hand in hand towards reaching that goal.

In February last year, I experienced a significant crisis when my father passed away. As such, I am now the man of the house. My family goes to the Meditation Centre and we have made many friends. I felt quite shocked when my father passed away, but I was able to cope with it well. I'm so surprised. I did not cry, instead I sat still and concentrated my mind at the centre of my body. Then, I found the answer. I realised that I had to be strong and face the facts of life. To be born, to grow old, to fall sick and die — these are the inevitable processes of life. Now, I encourage people around me to meditate and share merit to all my deceased family members.



Presently, my friends and I plan to organise meditation sessions in Saitama. We want to establish a new meditation centre here in the near future. I would like to see many people in this area to be given the opportunity to participate in activities and practise meditation. I think I would like to introduce simple meditation techniques to common Japanese, so they will understand. I want to see people join together as one, and I want to see everybody smiling with joy. I will do anything to achieve those smiles of happiness. And I believe that if everybody meditates regularly, they will find true happiness in life.

**Dr. Aaron Stern, Ph.D (U.S.A.)**



"My two daughters were born during my doctoral program and despite the joy they gave both my wife and I, all parents know the amount of time and energy required for child-rearing. Meditation helped me maintain my patience when handling the strain of a temper tantrum, a near sleepless night tending to a sick child and many other responsibilities associated with parenthood."

My introduction to *Dhammakaya* meditation began about five years ago when I first learned about the basic method from a monk at the Meditation Center of Chicago. I had meditated many years earlier using *Vipassana* meditation (essentially focusing on my breath) and had not returned to any regular meditation practice until learning about *Dhammakaya* meditation. I did some background reading and directed questions at various monks and people knowledgeable about the *Dhammakaya* method before starting to practice it regularly.

Similar to other people who had their minds consumed by the vicissitudes and influences of daily life, it was not easy to meditate initially. A key element of the *Dhammakaya* method was to empty the mind, clear out mental clutter and let the mind become still. A mind trained to "multi-task" (a good description of my mind) needs time to slow down so that it will not wander from thought to thought, memory to memory and worry to worry. I struggled with this mental wandering (and still do) for many months before I experienced my first moment of true mental stillness. That brief moment demonstrated the happiness associated with a still mind: a sense of being relaxed and at peace with the world, without feeling the need to escape from the world. I continued to meditate, although I felt a little annoyed on some days at my wandering mind.



There were also physical concerns with meditation. In my initial efforts to meditate, my legs would go numb and my back would start to ache. Monks recommended that I stretch regularly, especially before meditating, and this helped substantially. I also found I could greatly reduce my back pain by sitting with my back against a hard surface and lodging a small pillow against my lower back. Once I had addressed my physical discomfort, my meditation sessions grew longer and more relaxing.

Initially, I did nearly all my meditation at home. I was fortunate to have the opportunity in July 2005 to participate in Wat Phra Dhammakaya's Dhammadayada International Ordination program in Thailand. The monk instructors at the temple focused heavily on meditation practice, and all participants in the program meditated for at least four hours per day. The combination of concentrated meditation, along with the benefits of having regular access to highly experienced monks in *Dhammakaya* meditation, helped me progress notably. It felt very good to meditate and sometimes, I would see a small point or ball of light floating in front of me, something I had rarely perceived in my meditation at home. Even the memory of such experiences can help induce a feeling of contentment and help make future meditation efforts more fulfilling.



Meditation has had a number of tangible benefits in my life and my family life. I took up *Dhammakaya* meditation while I was in my doctoral program. Meditation reduced the intense stress associated with simultaneously completing my doctoral dissertation, teaching 40-50 undergraduate students, and searching for a job. It became important to me to find the time to meditate, typically early in the morning or late at night. Without meditation, I could have easily succumbed to the pressure of my responsibilities as a student and simply given up pursuing the doctorate, even after investing so much time and money. Instead, I found that meditation helped me to concentrate when writing my dissertation. My teaching improved also, as shown by the higher scores on teaching evaluations written by my students.



My two daughters were born during my doctoral program and despite the joy they gave both my wife and myself, all parents know the heavy amount of time and energy required for child-rearing. Meditation helped me maintain my patience when handling the strain of a temper tantrum, a near sleepless night tending to a sick child and many other responsibilities associated with parenthood.

Meditation also improved my relationship with my wife. I would often forget things, make wrong turns while driving, bump into objects and commit other errors that frustrated my wife because they occurred too frequently. Meditation improved my mental clarity, reducing the frequency of these blunders. I also had a tendency to think too much about myself, focusing on my own problems and priorities when the concerns needing the most attention were with my family. Meditation has made me more aware of what matters most in life and led me to stop and consider the consequences of my choices in my studies, work, and family.



In addition to the benefits of *Dhammakaya* meditation, various monks recommended practicing "loving-kindness meditation". Loving-kindness meditation involves mentally identifying and sending good wishes to all fellow human beings and creatures. When done consistently, it cultivates a sense of caring and compassion for one's living companions on the planet. Loving-kindness meditation helped shake me out of my penchant for putting my own needs above those of others, especially those of my family. Whenever I meditate now, I devote some time to loving-kindness meditation as an integral component of *Dhammakaya* meditation.



The more I have meditated, the more I have realized that the human mind is strong but very susceptible to influences that may weaken its powers of concentration and clarity. *Dhammakaya* meditation helped me see the value of keeping the mind relatively free of unnecessary clutter and other things that may impede this clarity. This is an important reason why I decided to stop consuming alcohol because I started to find that even small amounts – say, one bottle of beer – made my mind fuzzier than I expected. The alcohol buzz soon lost its attractiveness. My decision greatly pleased my wife as well and I hope it will serve as a good example for my children.

Meditation is an activity that everyone in this world should take part in. It is one of the few human activities free of any drawbacks. It is free, relaxing and good for the mind. It promotes improved behavior and according to an increasing amount of research, it has medical benefits such as lowering blood pressure. Meditation does not need to be a religiously-motivated activity in order to reap its advantages. Meditation only requires a commitment of time and some perseverance. The only case in which I would question the appropriateness of meditation is for a person with a serious mental illness or psychosis. Otherwise, there is every reason to believe that meditation has substantial potential for improving the quality of life for all living creatures by increasing the capacity of human beings to feel more relaxed, mentally alert, and at peace with themselves. And if people feel at peace with themselves, they will feel at peace with the world; something our planet direly needs.

# *Chapter 4*

# Knowledge and Career

“We can work, study, or have a family, but we should never neglect meditation. To do so would be the desertion from the way of true happiness and success in life. A peaceful state of mind will evolve and purify our thoughts so that we think thoroughly, speak pleasantly and act effectively.”

**Luang Phaw Dhammajayo**

## A Vessel of Knowledge

While we are all born with a mind and a body, and we live in a similar environment, haven't we all wondered why there are so many differences in abilities and talents among people? In fact, there are several factors accounting for our different abilities from one another. One important factor we cannot overlook is meditation. The mind is the foundation of all abilities and actions. Meditation will bring great benefits to us by not only helping to improve the efficiency of our actions, but also by helping to connect our minds with the centre point of the body. If we can bring our minds to a standstill at that centre, we will gain access to the source of all wholesome thought, speech and acts which will bring happiness and success to our lives.

Meditation will lead us to success in both the material world and the spiritual world. In the material world, whenever we are about to perform a deed, we should stop and think first. Meditate, then think, speak and act. For a car to run safely, its engine needs to be maintained. Meditation is like maintaining and fine-tuning your mind. **When the mind is skilled in meditation, learning becomes easier. It is as if we are a clean and open vessel able and ready to receive knowledge.**



## *Vitamin for the Mind*

In addition to the benefits that meditation brings to learning, it also helps to balance us as we pursue a career. Work creates a large amount of stress and anxiety which can lead to ill health. To work at a job which makes you miserable day after day, is against the principles of leading a correct life in this world.

**We should find satisfaction with our profession. We should come home pleased, not exhausted or depressed. The demands of a career and the development of the mind should be in balance.** Meditation can help with this aspect. It helps improve our efficiency and attitude. This can be compared to our bodies that will function more properly when they receive the appropriate vitamins. Meditation is the vitamin for our minds, so they can perform more efficiently, with more stability and at a higher capacity.

**We can work, study, or have a family, but we should never neglect meditation. To do so would be the desertion of the way to true happiness and success in life. A peaceful state**

**of mind will evolve and purify our thoughts so that we think thoroughly, speak pleasantly and act effectively.**

We should always visualise a meditation object, such as a crystal sphere, placing the mind at the seventh base of the body everyday, all day during our daily tasks or at work. It seems difficult to do all of this at the same time, but if we practise it regularly, it will become very easy. It is comparable to driving, which requires the coordination of both feet, both hands, both ears, the eyes and the brain. We can do a lot of things at the same time, so there is no excuse for not performing the duties of mind, in bringing to mind the crystal sphere and silently repeating our mantra during our daily tasks. We can do this, even when we are studying, working, or doing chores around the house. While we are working we can think about the crystal sphere, even casually, and after much practice, we will be able to visualise it clearly just as easily and naturally as the eyes can see or the ears can hear. If we can practise in this way, we will keep our minds happy and healthy while we are studying or working, and achieve success in both the material world and the spiritual world.



Many people who practise meditation are very successful in their careers and studies. Their stories will be shared as examples. These persons have successfully applied meditation in their lives, enjoying the success and happiness it brought them.

**Mr. Anant Asavabhokhin (Thailand)**



"When I brought meditation to my work life, everything changed. In the past, I always attempted to perform at the level of one hundred percent. But when I spoke, I could accomplish only half of what I wanted; and when I attempted to implement my ideas, I accomplished even less. But once I gained control over my mind, everything changed. When my goal was to perform at one hundred percent, I was able to achieve twice as much while talking, and far more in results."

I am a son in a Chinese family. My family owned a trading company. My family was never interested in Buddhism or meditation. We never went to any temple, never hung an amulet and never prayed at a spiritual shrine. What my family and I paid respect to were only the pictures of grandma, grandpa and shrines of our ancestors. I entered the faculty of engineering at the university. People in this faculty believe in their ability to control their own destiny with a brain and two hands. Then, I thought that the world was created by these engineers, and that they were more intelligent than the rest of mankind. I truly believed this and I remembered having a party at home with several friends after graduation and stole 16 bottles of my father's liquor.

During that time, there were no restraints in my life as I saw myself as having great knowledge, intelligence and willpower. Everything supported me in this belief because I had been successful at work — I opened my own company called 'Land and House' and managed to make it the top home sales company in Thailand. This made me even more confident that "one brain and two hands" could define this world.



At the end of 1994, I was persuaded by one of my employees to visit the Wat Phra Dhammakaya. I was given an opportunity to pay homage and to meet Luang Phaw Dhammajayo. That day, I asked many questions on Buddhism, and Luang Phaw Dhammajayo suggested me to read the Dhamma books and the Tripitaka. He told me that the answers to the questions I asked were in there. Later, I studied the books which he suggested. After reading them for a while, I started to wonder. I was shocked to read the story of infinite universes in the Tripitaka. How could it be? How could monks have known about this science? Humans only knew about this less than 100 years ago when Mr. Edwin Hubble looked through a telescope and found that what he saw was not only a myriad of stars but another universe. Before Hubble's discovery, humans only knew that they lived in the Milky Way, which consisted of 200 million stars. The eyes of humans, even with the aid of telescopes, could never see anything beyond this, much less dream of the infinite universes. Humans believed that there were nothing beyond this and never dreamed there were infinite universes. Once I read about this in the Tripitaka, I was shocked about how those who wrote the Tripitaka around 2,000 years ago knew about the infinite universes.

By studying continuously, I started to get the answers I had been seeking. In the meantime, I kept coming to the temple, learning Dhamma, reading the Tripitaka, listening to the sermons, and practising meditation. I started to absorb and understand meditation and merit gradually. Finally, I accepted the task of being the leader of Maha Dhammakaya Cetiya (The Great Dhammakaya Pagoda) construction and continued to come to the temple.

Then, in 1997, as the chairman and CEO of Land and House Public Company Limited, I faced an enormous financial crisis caused by the devaluation of the Thai currency. I had to confront the worst crisis of my life. The company and its Home Pro Company lost money from the reduced baht value. Investments depreciated. The stock value of Land and House Company decreased a 100 times from the high value of 800 baht to 8 baht only. Moreover, I got into trouble, not because I fled my own debt, but because I had pledged for someone else.

Between 1998 to 1999, many problems beset me severely. My company lost money. Creditors dunned me to pay my many debts. I was accused. I was deeply troubled as my child might not be able to complete his education abroad. I was very depressed. I was so afraid of not having money, being thought disreputable, and not being capable of paying my debts. At that time, I felt that I could not do anything even though I had millions of baht in my personal bank account. I thought of allowing the company to go bankrupt. But I did not do it — I could not bear seeing the company I built with my hands fall apart in front of me. I could not bear seeing hundreds of my employees who had worked together with me for years become jobless. I made the decision to fight. I did not lay off any employees. However, under the pressure of so many debts, I could not increase their salaries. I withdrew my own money and increased the investment required to support the company. I negotiated with foreign lenders to extend their limits. Over time, I resolved the problems one by one.



I can truly say that I could pass through that difficult time successfully because of meditation. At the time of troubles, I was so distraught because I faced problems in every direction I turned. It was good that I still had my great teacher, Luang Phaw Dhammajayo, as my pillar and model. He always reminded me to close my eyes, be comfortable, stay still, spread the loving kindness, and then think of all the deeds of merit I had performed. It seems so simple, but it is incredibly helpful. It is the key to the method which offers a perfect solution.

Luang Phaw Dhammajayo used to tell me that perfect wisdom has never come from the anxious mind. Hence, whenever I found myself worrying too much, I was determined to forget about my troubles by meditating and clearing my mind. I began to stop worrying so much about my problems. I began to see that no matter how difficult my problems were, the world would not end there and then if I could not solve them immediately.

Whenever I was under pressure, meditation helped me control my emotions better. For example, I had to negotiate the debts with my creditors. They complained to me a lot, but I did not respond. I smiled, stayed calm, and did not say anything. I kept my mind calm as Luang Phaw Dhammajayo taught. Then, my creditors told me that I was a polite and patient debtor. They did not know what I was thinking when I just kept smiling without saying a word. They thought I was being clever. In fact, what I was doing was meditating with open eyes. I did not think of anything else.



When I brought meditation to my work life, everything changed. In the past, I always attempted to perform at the level of 100 percent. But when I spoke, I could accomplish only half of what I wanted; and when I attempted to implement my ideas, I accomplished even less. But once I gained control over my mind, everything changed. When my goal was to perform at 100 per cent, I was able to achieve twice as much while talking, and far more in results. Previously, I often had eight meetings a day and because of the many morning meetings, I had two breakfasts on some days. Now, I work less and experience an increase in productivity and am not so tired as before. But the result is an increase in production.



What is amazing was that meditation helped me in being creative and intuitive. One example was the Land and House Company's "Ready-Before-Sale" project. Another example was a price strategy for the Home Pro Company. These ideas came to me after meditating. They did not occur to me at first. When I cleared my mind during meditation, I thought of what I had never thought of in the past. The answers came to my mind unexpectedly.

I could not think of those at first. But after meditation, I cleared my mind and thought of what I had never thought of in the past. The answers came across my mind unexpectedly. After that, facing the problems became much simpler. The solutions were so simple that I had never thought of them. When I tried to implement those solutions, the results were far greater than the ideas I had brainstormed about in meetings. Indeed, facing more problems became much simpler through meditation.



In the case of the Land and House Company, it became clear to me, after mediation, that the company has been in the real estate business for 30 years and it needed to get out of the cyclical ups and downs. Unlike industries based on intuitive technologies such as microchip, biotechnology or nanotechnology, our business was a boring one. The only technology we have is bricking and rendering, which has been the same for a thousand years. Even though we constantly attempt to create innovative styles for homes, within a week after completion, someone else will copy it.



What occurred to me from the meditation was how to keep a consistent quality. Let's think of the car assembly manufacture: car manufacturers have to finish assembling and implement quality control before selling. In Thai real estate, it was a norm to first build a few model homes and wait for orders before building the real homes; which meant clients have the opportunity to walk into the manufactured product, check the belt of the car, and ask to change the colour of the door, seat, etc. I decided that we must build all the standard homes before attempting to sell them, like the method of the car assembly manufacture.

This idea occurred to me in 2000 to 2001. I called about 10 executives into a meeting and announced my idea. I told them that I would build a finished home before selling. I would let go of the old way. All the ten executives disagreed with my idea. I had to coerce them to do it until, gradually, they started to believe in my idea. They, then, went on show this method to hundreds of other employees.



Likewise, nobody believed the effectiveness of this method and they did not want to do it. My company is reasonably liberal: I distribute the power to every employee to allow them to have control over their financial future and I let them make decisions to buy the land on their own. If their decisions benefit the company, they will benefit the employees as well. They were hence concerned that if they followed my idea, the company might be in bad shape and they did not want to implement it. It was difficult to get the employees to work on the project. But, as time went on, the project yielded positive results. It turned Land and House Company from a 45 thousand million baht loss into a profitable business. The most profitable year was in 2003 when our profit went up to an unprecedented 6,000 million baht. I received a dividend of 2,000. With half of it, I managed to clear all debts. I also made charitable donations with a part of the dividend.



The Home Pro company, the affiliate of the Land and House Company, has been established for more than 10 years. I began the company because I wanted to provide customers greater convenience. Previously, once customers bought their houses, they had to go to different warehouses themselves to select their furniture.

In 1997, we had three branches. I wanted to open more branches but the business only made a small profit. One day after meditating, I got an idea. I talked to my manager: "Could we not expand the branches"? He told me that it was difficult to expand as we made only one percent profit. If we sold a thousand million baht a year, we will only receive 10 million baht profit. This was because we had a policy of "Low Price Every Day". I asked him "May I beg your pardon? Why do we have to be 'Low Price Every Day'? In fact, we don't even have competitors. We are a store for convenience, not a discount store. When you buy here, you get everything you need. But we never claim that our stores have the cheapest price. We are going to sell with the close price to our competitors or even a higher price but the customers are coming to us for convenience."

I cancelled the advertisements "Low Price Every Day" and changed it to "We have lots of choices for you" and "We return your money if you found a cheaper price". For example, we have 300 styles of handles and 400 styles of knobs to choose from. When customers come to us, they can purchase everything in one place. Later on, I adjusted the price two more percent upwards. With this simple idea, our profit tripled in the next year and within five years, we expanded from three branches to 26 branches. And we plan to expand year after year.



Finally, I believe that in life, one has to face both positive and negative developments. If I may, I would like to offer this advice: no matter what you come across, don't worry. Clear your mind and meditate. By bringing joy to your mind, major worries will seem trivial. Problems will lessen.

**Mr. Andrew Cowan (U.S.A.)**

"I believe meditation has helped with my work and allowed me to have empathy with other people. I feel that, by meditating, I have been able to more fully understand myself. This has allowed me to fully relate with patients, many of whom have problems which go beyond disease, and enter into the realm of the mind."

I first found out about the Dhammakaya Meditation Center in Seattle, Washington State, while working at the hospital in a clinic. The person who invited me to the center was Sunan Yesuwan, who worked at the front desk. She invited me to come and teach English to the monks that stayed at the meditation center she attended. I agreed, and first came to the center in October, 2002. One of the staff at the center kept telling me I should meditate. The most noticeable effect that meditation had on me when I started, was that I became calmer and relaxed in every day life and it also contributed to a general decrease in my anxiety level, So, I decided that this was the most worthwhile activity. I continued meditating, and started coming to meditate with Luang Phaw Dhammajayo at the center every Saturday evening.

In the past, I used to have some personality characteristics that were maladaptive. I used to be much more irritable, easily angered, bad-tempered and moody. Meditation has helped to improve these problems. My parents first noted that I was a much nicer person to be with after I had been meditating for some time. Because of meditation, I started to avoid drinking alcohol, even before I understood the five precepts. I felt that drinking alcohol made my meditation less clear, which led me to decrease and eventually stop drinking alcohol, after I learned more about Buddhist morality.

Another way in which meditation has helped me is that I have become less impulsive. In the past, I used to make decisions without thinking very much, or make reckless monetary purchases, without fully considering whether I needed them or not. Additionally, I would choose to spend time with friends at bars or concerts, even though I didn't want to go. After having meditated for some period of time, I have become less impulsive, and more careful about the decisions I make. In a word, I would say that I have become more *mindful* of what I am doing.



Meditation has also supported me in meeting good friends. Prior to coming to the meditation center, I had many friends who engaged in poor behaviors. Often, simply because I had known nothing else, I would spend time with these people and followed them drinking, going out late at night and engaging in other deleterious activities. When I started to meditate, I have been able to come to the center more often and this has brought me into contact with good friends and people who encouraged me to behave in the right way. I truly feel that meditation has allowed much of this to occur.

I strongly feel that meditation supports a healthier, lower stress life for people in the world today. It can help people feel less stressed and more relaxed in everyday life. Meditation can improve one's confidence in the world, because we can discover our own nature and ourselves better,. In my own experience, meditation has helped me to quit drinking alcohol, avoid bad friends and attain both personal and career achievements. I feel like I would not be in the position I am now, had I not started to practice meditation.

Meditation has also helped in my work. I am currently a medical student at the University of Washington in Seattle, Washington State, USA. Often times, when I am working with patients, the sufferings they must endure and the diseases they have affect us emotionally. When I take time to meditate, I am able to decrease this stress and not feel so sad anymore. As a doctor, it is important to be very aware of what is going on, and to pay attention to what is happening. I feel that meditation supports awareness, and helps me to better focus on details of a patient's appearance and case. I have noticed before that if I have not taken sufficient time for meditation, my thinking is less clear and work becomes harder.



One thing in particular that meditation has helped me with is my long working hours that sometimes pass without any breaks. Sometimes, I go to a quiet place, close my eyes, and imagine a crystal ball or a Buddha image at the center of my body. I do this until I feel peaceful, and then go back to work. It's truly amazing how rejuvenating and helpful this simple procedure is. I started to do this while on surgery, which, of all my "rotations" has the longest hours, and many times no sleep for long periods of time. Sometimes, I would want to sleep so much, but still had several hours of work to do before I could go home. I feel that my meditation practice helped me to endure those times.



In addition, one important aspect of working in surgery is being in the operating room. In the operating room, one very important concept is keeping "a sterile field". Basically, this means that once you have cleaned your arms and hands, and have put on gowns and gloves, you are "sterile". The patient is also sterile. Thus, one cannot "break the sterile field" by touching non-sterile objects, including your face, legs, or anything else but the patient. I feel that the sort of concentration and focus necessary to prevent breaking the sterile field is something which can be enhanced with meditation. Meditation practice helped me stay mindful while I am in the operating room, and not needlessly endanger the lives of patients by contaminating the sterile field.



Another thing that I believe meditation has helped with at my work is being able to have empathy with other people. I feel that, by meditating, I have been able to more fully understand myself. This has allowed me to fully relate with patients, many of whom have problems which go beyond disease, and enter into the realm of the mind. A large percentage of people who are at hospitals have co-existing mental illness. Thus, neither their minds nor their bodies are in good health. It's sometimes difficult to pick up on this subtlety, but I feel that my meditation practice has given me insight into this aspect of health care.

My current goal is to finish medical school and enter the field of surgery. Surgery is a tough and demanding field of medicine, and the hours are long and hard. However, the amount of good surgeons can do for people is amazing. I'm excited to enter this field of medicine, but still feel like something is missing from it. As a future doctor, I intend not only to treat the patient's diseases, but also to take care of their minds as well. I will incorporate this sort of theme, comprising mind and body health, into my future practice as a doctor.



As far as my own meditation experience goes, I have had some very good experiences during my meditation. On a couple of occasions, I've seen a bright light, brighter than the sun, at the center of my body. While this experience only lasted briefly, the feeling I had at the time was something which I can't describe. On other occasions, I've been able to clearly visualize a crystal ball at my center, and have felt very peaceful. One important aspect, for me, in my meditation, is that it has helped me to gain wisdom about situations in life. In many instances, I think that meditation has improved my wisdom about certain events and helped me to make better decisions regarding them.



If I could tell the people of the world anything, it is that meditation is one of the best activities for mental and physical health. I would also say that meditation is for everybody – not just for monks or Buddhists. Every religious background can experience the benefits of meditation. Meditation can help us deal with the stress of everyday life, and can also help us endure difficulties that we may encounter. More importantly, it can help us find a goal for our lives, and to better understand the true nature of things.

**Ms. Supatra Phuripanyo (Thailand)**



"I continued to meditate everyday. Day after day, others around me noticed a change in me. My boss asked what had happened; why was I not arguing with him as I had before? My subordinate asked me why I looked more relaxed and was easier to approach."

Five years ago, I had lymphatic cancer. The doctor said that I needed 11 chemotherapy and 36 radiation sessions. Before I began the three-month long treatment, the doctor used a CT scan to examine my body and found the formation of cancer cells which had formed into the shape of a string of beads. During the treatment, I began practising meditation two to three hours a day; I did not work full time.



What was really surprising was that I never had any side effects from the chemotherapy and radiation, unlike other patients who experienced vomiting, diarrhoea, and hair loss. I was able to smile, laugh and chat with the nurses, and had also encouraged other patients. The doctors and nurses were all surprised and said, "You look like a visitor rather than a patient." After the treatment, the doctor sent me for another CT scan again. The results were unbelievable because all of the cancer cells miraculously disappeared. It was as though they had never existed. The two doctors who gave me the chemotherapy were more surprised than I was.

To ensure that no mistake were made, the doctors re-examined my body, taking hundreds of x-rays. After the doctors examined every film, they were extremely surprised that the cancer cells had all disappeared. One of the doctors said, "This is a miracle." Another said, "You must have done a lot of good deeds. This is quite unusual." I told the doctors that this was because I had meditated and accumulated merit." Meditation helped me survive. Doctors can only treat the physical body, but patients need to treat their own mental body. Without meditation, patients can feel stressed and anxious; they can become more nervous and the symptoms can worsen. I was so glad to learn that the doctor proposed to the Hospital Board of Directors to provide meditation practice to patients, soon after.

The meditation experience that made an unforgettable impression on me was the meditation retreat at the Phu-kradueng National Park in Loei Province. I kept this memory fresh in my mind because it was when I met the first love of my life. I did not expect to attain the Dhamma within or be able to see anything while I was practising meditation there. I only thought that this was a form of relaxation for me to take a break from work. At that time, I worked as a financial controller, so I had many problems to think about. During the first two to three days of meditation, thoughts about work wandered into my mind from time to time. When I was able to still my mind and set aside work-related matters such as the numbers and the financial planning, I was able to remain in the stillness longer and transcend to a deeper level. Whenever distractions emerged, I ignored them and allowed them to pass.



During the week of meditation, I learned that I had to become a student or a child again and give up my analytical tendencies. Children tend to have no attitudes and are not likely to think ahead. There may be several exceptions, but that is due to not knowing much, so they tend to see people or matters without any defilements.

During that time, my mind reached a higher level of stillness. When I meditated, I would gently close my eyes and breathe in deeply, as far as my breath would go. I would take that point as the centre of my body and it was where I placed my mind. Soon, my mind would come to a standstill, so I would stop repeating the mantra and stop imagining an unclear crystal sphere. I felt that I was entering an inner world filled with happiness and peace. The lower part of my body became light and gradually disappeared from my mind. Suddenly, a bright light expanded from the centre of my body. The brightness, peace and happiness permeated throughout my body. It was a very good experience. While looking at the middle of the brightness, which happened to be also the brightest point, I was pulled into the centre point of the body. It felt like I was falling from a cliff. I was so frightened! When I opened my eyes, everything around me was still the same as before.

After that, I asked the monk instructor, who taught me how to meditate, for advice. He kindly advised me that my mind was about to reach the state of perfect stillness. Some people will feel like they are being pulled into their centre of gravity. He assured me that there was nothing to be frightened of or worried about. I should just observe peacefully until it passed, since it occurs naturally as our mind enters a purer realm of happiness and peacefulness. Although I was quite frightened by the experience of being pulled into the centre point of the body for the first time, I was delighted with the joy, peace of mind and happiness I had experienced and had never found before.



The next day, I told myself that I would not be frightened by the inner experience again and continued to meditate as I had done the day before. In a short while, I saw a small bright star, like a small spot that was visible in a sky without clouds. After that, I felt like I was falling into a tube. I tried to keep my mind still and observed what would happen next. Soon, I saw a bright light from a crystal ball the size of an orange. The crystal ball kept expanding until it covered my entire body. I felt secure, delighted, and comfortable in that crystal ball, as if it was my real home. Then, I felt my body lightened and disappeared until I was one with the air. I felt so happy that I could not possibly explain it in words. I considered it to be the happiest day of my life. It was the most beautiful, wonderful and most unforgettable experience.

When I returned to work, I continued to meditate everyday. Day after day, others around me noticed a change in me. My boss asked me what had happened. Why was I not arguing with him as I had before? My subordinate asked me why I looked more relaxed and was easier to approach. Before meditating, I would not give in to anyone, including my husband, because I made more money than him. But since then, I made a promise to myself to express any disagreement in a diplomatic manner and be more willing to compromise. After I practised more meditation, I smiled more often and spoke pleasantly to everyone. I was cautious of any words or actions that could affect others. Before I began practising meditation, I was concerned only with my own interests. I did not worry about whether my words would hurt others and I was like a cobra aiming to strike at those who disagreed with me, disobeyed me or did not comply with my orders.

Today, I am 100 percent confident that meditation is the important key to the success in my career and family life. On any day that I feel stressed, I will meditate. Even though I may see only darkness, at the very least I know that my mind will be at ease and I am able to find solutions to problems. Usually, I will have a notebook next to me to record the effective means to solve a problem. I will also record other creative thoughts that may arise after meditation, so that I will not forget.



Meditation helped to improve the capacity of my analytical skills. As I analysed problems with more consideration and creativity, I was promoted to General Manager. I now feel less stressed, and this was because I was less angry and smiled more often at work. My subordinates thanked me for allowing them to work at the office. I no longer force the sales team and verbally offend them in order to meet sales goals. Instead, I used pleasant words to motivate them to perform better and advised and directed them patiently. I found this way to be more effective, as more than 2,500 sales personnel began to work with their hearts rather than for their monthly pay check. The courage and inspiration of my subordinates have gradually increased, and the company's profits had grown continuously.



My husband and my two sons noticed that I was happier and smiled more often. They were surprised with the change that they saw in me. They wondered how a businesswoman like me had the time to and was willing to meditate an hour each day. I told them that I had found life's answer in meditation. In the end, every family member began to practise meditation. They became more calm and patient. We listened more and showed more interest in each other. My husband was happy to see that I became more jovial. He once told me that I looked younger because I smiled more often. Our family never experienced this kind of happiness before. My boss told me I was by far luckier than the first prize winner of a lottery, because money cannot buy a happy family.



Every day, I meditate for about an hour. When I close my eyelids to meditate, I always see brightness. Sometimes I feel that my whole body totally disappears and is one with the natural environment. No matter how it is, I am happy every time I meditate. I feel freedom and enjoy the peace and tranquility that arise. The happiness from meditation cannot be compared to any sort of happiness from the material world, such as the happiness that comes from having a new car, a new house, or a higher position at work. External wealth arises with responsibility, anxiety, and problems. I once told a friend of mine, who was also a manager, by saying that, "Money can buy a car, but it cannot buy happiness for the owner sitting in that car". He agreed that a new car and a higher post did not make him happy at all. Instead, it made him feel more stressed and anxious.



Before, when I earned one million baht, I wanted to have five million baht. When I earned five million baht, I wanted to have ten million baht. After I achieved it, I enjoyed it for a short while, like I was chasing the shadow of happiness, but I never really attained true happiness. Meditation is the best cure for the modern world's illness, which includes stress, anxiety and even boredom. It is considered a means for self-treatment, a form of relaxation that everyone can achieve. You do not need to have money in order to meditate; just gently close your eyes, still your mind and feel happy. Only you can do this for yourself.

**Ms. Margitta Dietermann (Switzerland)**



"Meditation makes me calm and compassionate, which also makes people around me feel better. Meditation gives me the power of patience and stability even in a phase of emotional ups and downs."

I am Margitta Dietermann and I am 48 years old. I was born in Germany and I left my country with my own young family when I was 26 years old. For more than 22 years now, I'm living and studying in Switzerland, staying close to the city of Zurich in a lively town with an increasing number of inhabitants.



I'm a psychotherapist and private teacher. Before I started meditation I felt discouraged to run my own business, asking myself: *'Who am I that people would ask especially for* ***my*** *help? There are hundreds of therapists, why would any person call* ***just me****?'* According to that personal style of thinking, my business was not very successful and for six years I even was not able to earn my own living.

I urgently was longing for knowledge and wisdom to guide myself and other people in a decent way, but I didn't believe in my own abilities. Since I learned how to meditate, I changed my opinion about myself. I realised that I am full of love and high potential and I asked myself: *'What is my special gift that I can bring to people in society'?*



I do freelance work and have been doing so for more than ten years. I'm working with singles, couples and families in consulting sessions and creative workshops. One aspect of my work is to support people to overcome their psychic problems in their personal, family and social life and to help them to reveal by themselves their individual and unique mission in life. People who are asking me for help are suffering from different symptoms, for example from anxiety, anger, dissatisfaction in life, depression, physical dysfunctions, burning out symptoms and different stages of inner and outer conflicts, mainly showing up in their partnerships and families – with the result of broken hearts, broken families, broken relationships – both private and job-related.



An important part of my profession is to teach parents how to get along with their children and how to raise them in a sympathetic, responsible and ethical way, which means also to train themselves as parents in understanding their own responsibilities and being a good role model. Without healthy relationships, we will have an unmanageable problem in society in the near future.

To understand the principle of cause and effect in life is of prime importance to me. How to avoid doing bad and how to do good deeds – this seems to be the most important subject in life for me. This is also really interesting for my profession, because it concerns relationships. It can really help us to understand and to accept situations more deeply, to stop blaming others and to start developing our own potential of love and success in life.



I have to be alert and wise, in order to know where to find the root problem and how to encourage person to look at the very reason that causes his problem. Nobody likes to look at the person in the mirror. Therefore, it's necessary for me to find the right words and questions – an artful speech — so that people may find their own answers. This activity calls for the highest concentration. Meditation enables me to acquire and improve the quality of my power of concentration.

I aim to provide the right climate so that people can make their own choices to change their life actively for the better. According to experience, a personal choice for a new concept in life is the most encouraging way to proceed in breaking bad habits of thinking, speaking and acting – which regularly leads to the dissatisfaction in people's lives.



I try to encourage people to trust their own strength and skills. They first have to know them. So, I have to find ways to lead them to discover their inner potential. I intend to inspire people to create their own personal guideline to follow in their daily life which leads them to more inner peace and happiness. I have to be careful in order not to increase their inner resistance against helpful solutions, and to diminish resistance against following an ethical lifestyle.

Necessarily, I myself have to be a good role model as a teacher – otherwise no one will follow my suggestions. How could I manage that without meditation? Meditation makes me calm and compassionate, so that people around me feel better. Meditation gives me the power of patience and stability even in a phase of emotional ups and downs. As a result, my customers are able to hold on and stay the course even if they feel unsure of themselves and harbour doubts.



Meditation stimulates my intuition and creativity. People I am working with often report about their newly detected creativity. While meditating, I discovered that I had never shown love and appreciation to my parents that I feel for all beings inside during and after meditation sessions. I started doing so. As a result of this, the majority of my customers are able to give up their resistance against their own parents, spouse or children. A lot of them meet the challenge of developing solutions even for the 'hottest' conflict.

A precondition for teaching a new lifestyle in the society I live in seems to be offering people innovative and creative workshops and to design appealing workshop sessions. I have to train myself in teaching the various topics of highest interest, e.g., for parents or couples. I'm working to present basic knowledge of how to find inner peace and social success to worldly people with different educational levels.



Meditation allows me to experience by myself the highest level of peace inside I ever knew. I had no idea before that I was capable of feeling so happy! As a result of this, the majority of my customers are getting interested in meditation – no matter what their educational level.

Simultaneously they are talking about the fast improvement of their family members while they are working on adopting their own new attitude of life. It's amazing. It is wonderful to hear so much positive feedback of my work even in such short periods of time.

Necessarily, I have to organise my business, to plan the structure of one month, six months, one year and so on. Additionally, there is a lot of intensive work like managing the budget, public relations, acquiring new customers, communicating information, promoting myself as well as enlarging and improving my knowledge. Each time I get tired of meeting all demands, I sit, slow down and meditate to find new vital energy and courage. Only few minutes of practising can change my existential orientation for the better.

Since I started to meditate, I found the calm and happiness I was looking for. Since I practised meditation, I know exactly about my light, my power and my talents. To know exactly how gifted I am, it gives me the feeling of being worthy to be alive and being able to help people to discover their own treasures and resources inside themselves. I feel more powerful and strong and healthy.

The most amazing miracle is that I am able to improve and enlarge my own professional activities. I get enquires regarding very interesting business projects and I dare to meet a challenge.

Consequently, my income has increased like never before. I changed my home and business residence to a more beautiful and comfortable one. It's a calm and bright apartment in an enjoyable neighbourhood. The place is near the lake of Zurich and well connected to public transport, so that people can reach me easily.



But my life is getting rich not only with money. Something very important happened to me. Unlike my past, I now experience peace with all my family members and friends. I succeeded in practising true friendship with different people. In short, I'm never missing anything I need for my life; instead I can start giving myself.

I would like to encourage everybody to meditate, because you will feel healthier, wealthier and more successful in your life. Meditation can help you find the way to reach your biggest goal in life. You will get satisfaction and joy. Everything you are looking for – you will find not outside, but inside yourself. No one can give you the object of your greatest desire but you: your own pure inner light. It's already within your self! Just detect it – by starting to meditate! It is the most exciting adventure in life to get in touch with your own original root power.



## *How I started*

It was in 1996, when I first became interested in meditation. My husband was a good example for me. After starting to meditate continuously every day, he changed to be calmer, more flexible and patient. He liked meditation so much that he learned from his teacher how to teach students. Thus, I got curious about meditation and I registered in one of my husband's classes in order to learn it. He was a good teacher. But I could not deal with the method and I gave up.

Two years later in 1998, I met another teacher and learned a new method to meditate. She trained me first to focus on my heart in order to find the 'entrance' for a deeper level, then to rest at a point below the navel. I tried hard but could not deal with this method as well. However, while practising, I realised that I knew by myself a place inside my body which attracted my attention. Within that point between my navel and my heart, I felt comfortable and peaceful. It's the place I am in contact with, to 'catch' my perception or intuition.

Since then I tried to find my own way to meditate: I gently closed my eyes and concentrated on my breathing to get deeper. With my inner eye, I 'travelled' through my body in order to relax all tensions. I observed my breathing continuously while trying to let go of all thoughts. This exercise gave me the feeling of regeneration and peace.



In 2002, I had the biggest breakdown in my life that I had ever experienced. I just got divorced from my second husband. During this time, my method of meditation kept me grounded and prevented me from depression.

One year later, in 2003, I met a most impressive Swiss lady, Elsbeth, who became my teacher and friend as well. She taught me how to meditate with ease. I felt convenient from the very first beginning, because she told me: 'just do 'nothing' - simply be happy'!

I started to work with her to reorganise my broken life. Elsbeth helped me to discover the root causes of my suffering. And she taught me the basic *Dhammakaya* technique to meditate. I realised that I knew the special point in my body to calm my mind already. But it took time for me to learn to stay at the certain place within – called the 7$^{th}$ base of the body – but it felt great. Although I could not see anything, I felt calm, light and very peaceful.



## *Personal Techniques*

The first time when I began the Dhammakaya Meditation method: I was sitting on the floor on a 10 cm high and round meditation cushion in the half lotus position or kneeling with my lower legs turned back. I straightened up my back and with smoothly closed eyes, I began to breathe more slowly and deeply. First, I concentrated on the relaxation of all muscles in my body. Afterward, I tried to visualise a clear bright object like a small crystal ball – small like the tip of my smallest finger - and I allowed myself to let it enter into my body. I automatically felt a warm and tingling feeling in the zone of my solar plexus, but I didn't see any crystal ball or light.



I was disappointed. Through days and weeks, I tried too hard. In the beginning, I was only able to sit 20 to 30 minutes, than my knees started hurting. When I was participating in my first seven-day meditation retreat in Chiang Mai, north of Thailand, I felt more pain in my body than progress in my meditation. After realising that I forced my body and my mind, I simply focused on relaxing and the feeling of happiness arose each time I got deeper inside. At the same time, I noticed that I didn't see any light, but I had the feeling of sitting in a sphere of light and perfect harmony.

After a year, the pain in my knees ultimately caused me to change my position and I had to sit on a chair. I always changed from chair to floor for short meditation sessions to let my body get accustomed and it worked! After two years, I was able to sit comfortably in the half lotus position, the right leg across the left leg. Now, I am able to sit for one to two hours without pain.



## *How I proceeded*

With the help of the Teaching Monks, I learned how to guide my mind through the seven key points of the body and how to still my mind at the seventh base - two finger-breadths above the navel level - in my very centre. I use the mantra 'Samma Arahang' (which means 'purify the mind') repeating silently three times at each key point, until resting my mind at the seventh base. By doing so, I have the feeling of efficiently closing the door to my outer sensual perception and to open up the door to my world of peace within. In case of a wondering mind, this mantra brings me back to settle my mind again and again in my centre. I use it often during my daily work as well, in order to 'reset' the activity of my mind. I am able to experience instantaneous happiness only by remembering it.



Sometimes, I notice in the beginning of my meditation session that my mind is willing to settle down. If this happens, I let it go straight to the seventh base, without travelling through all key points of my body. I always keep reciting the silent mantra 'Samma Arahang' until it disappears by itself. From this moment on, I feel profound happiness and joy.

In the beginning, it was difficult for me to sit down regularly each day, until I cultivated my discipline with a structured plan of my day. This gave me the chance to answer my basic need for tranquility and happiness, which now allows me to sit down and meditate with joy!

If my brain is too active and if I have uncountable thoughts or some resistance to sitting down, I try to do the walking meditation for half an hour in the forest and fields nearby. After returning home, I feel refreshed and for the most part I can sit down and slow down.

By meditating in the group and by training with the Teaching Monks, I always get inspired to exercise meditation regularly at home, each day at least 30 minutes in the morning and 30 minutes in the evening; if possible I would increase the period of meditation time to one hour or more for each session.



We have one slogan in our Swiss Team: SIT DOWN – SLOW DOWN – at least:

- once a day;
- once a week in a group;
- once a month (overnight – each First Sunday);
- once a year (one-week retreat); and
- after 3 years of daily meditation give yourself the inspirational treatment of a one-month meditation retreat.

## *Particular approach*

I like the lotus flower. It seems to be the most beautiful flower for me. I have a lotus flower crafted from crystal with a clear crystal ball on the top. I like to visualise the crystal ball on the top of this crystal lotus flower in the centre of my body. It opens to me symbolically as the entrance to my own crystal world inside. I just feel bright, beautiful and pure by observing it. In this moment, it's easier for me to concentrate and to calm my mind, because I do it with so much joy!



I try to be connected daily via the internet to the DMC programme and the teachings of the Most Venerable Abbot Luang Phaw Dhammajayo. I like to join in the meditation with teaching monks and the *Dhammakaya* students all over the world at the same time. In this way, I feel happier than if I were meditating alone.

After finishing meditation, I was so delighted. I felt pure and perfect happiness. I retained this happiness for the following days. I felt such a deep and lively connection to the inner body; something unlike what I had ever experienced before. It was an endless stream of power which arises from inside meant to be shared with every being.

# Chapter 5

# Hope and Willpower

"Whenever we are sad, dealing with a loss or a disappointment that causes sorrow and distress, we can meditate to keep our mind calm, focused and positive as well as to provide us with the willpower to continue. It is a willpower derived from the purest form of wisdom that can help us clearly comprehend the truth of life and the way of the world."

**Luang Phaw Dhammajayo**

## *Source of Willpower*

We are born as human beings and it is natural that we have to confront both positive and negative changes throughout our lives. No matter what economic or social situation we come from, there are equal chances that we will experience a crisis in our lives. Suffering is the constant for all humankind; everyone has to deal with one problem or another regardless of whether it is big or small. These problems could range from thwarted desires to being separated from people or things we love. These unfortunate events occur throughout our lives, causing distress and discouragement.



**Some people turn to drugs, alcohol, gambling or other distractions to temporarily forget their unhappiness. Resorting to these**

**things is not the correct way to resolve one's problems. If we have to face misfortune over and over again, we would have to go through the same distress because our minds lack the proper fortitude. Since we cannot keep adversity from finding us, we can strengthen the mind against despair and depression. Meditation is a great way to help us develop the iron willpower to confront emotions and thoughts that make us weak.**



As soon as we attain inner happiness from meditation, the mind will be strong. Its fortitude comes from a wisdom derived from our pure inner selves. As we continue keeping our minds calm and focused at the centre of the body, we will experience an internal awakening. We will be able to understand the truth of life thoroughly and consequently change our behavior in a positive way. We will resolve to lead a life that is pure in action, speech, thought, devoid of grief, sadness, resentment and regrets. **Therefore, when we focus our minds in the centre of our bodies, we will feel more joy compared to if we focused on our worries. When our minds are clouded with worry, we cannot free ourselves from distress. We attach our minds to those things and bring them back to us. However, when our minds focus on the inner crystal sphere, we will feel contentment and leave all other things behind.**

## *Overcoming a Crisis with a Calm Mind*

Meditation will help us understand and come to terms with the loss of a loved one. With wisdom, we learn that loss is natural. Meditation provides the strength and wisdom to escape sadness and begin a new chapter in our lives.

We must maintain our willpower to live and continue performing good deeds no matter what happens. Therefore, we must be prepared to face anything. **If we practise meditation until we achieve good results, we will have the hope and willpower to move ahead. We will be happy and cheerful even when unfortunate circumstances such as illness, unemployment, loss of loved ones, financial crisis, accidents or family problems afflict us. Our minds will be calm, thoughtful and ready to overcome any crisis peacefully and gracefully.**

**Ms. Pat Goski (U.S.A.)**



"Sometimes while I meditate, I can feel a tremendous flow of loving-kindness within me. When spreading this loving-kindness and good wishes limitlessly to everyone and everywhere, I can feel the warm-heartedness that it creates. Meditation has helped me find loving-kindness, healing, and peace."

My name is Pat Goski. I am a 52 year-old American working as a registered nurse. I was raised in the Catholic tradition, converted to a more fundamental type of Christianity and have studied the Bible extensively. I was relatively happy with my life and family and had a stable career. Then, on 27 November, 2004, my beloved son was killed in an accident. It was such a great loss that it was impossible to describe the depth of pain which I experienced! I felt as though a nuclear bomb had exploded in my life, and there I was, standing alone in the devastation of what 'used to be' my life. As though losing my beloved child was not enough, I lost two jobs over the course of eight months. I lost my income and several friends, and was almost kicked out of my residence. My life was filled with tears, pain and devastation. During this very difficult time, I continued to pray and meditate occasionally.

In the beginning of 2005, someone urged me to meditate consistently, saying that he believed meditation would be the key to my healing. Indeed, it was. The following summer, I was referred to the Dhammakaya meditation center in New Jersey.



Upon my arrival at the New Jersey Meditation Center, the monks were already reciting their evening chantings. (It was a Tuesday night, - one of the two times per week that a guided meditation in English was offered to the public.) As soon as I sat down, I felt like I had returned to my true home. From that day onwards, I continued meditating and began to have an interest in Buddhism.

I started meditation in a simple way, sitting in a relaxed and comfortable posture, keeping my eyes closed, easily and gently. I felt serene and relaxed. By just following the voice of the venerable one, I was happy. A smile appeared on my face automatically. If thoughts intruded during the meditation, I repeated the mantra "Samma Arahang" in my mind. Within seconds, I was again serene and calm. It was so calming that I felt like everything around me was clear and transparent. I felt so inexplicably happy! Often, I felt as though I was being 'drawn' deeper inside of myself. The deeper I went, the clearer everything became! I 'let it be', and saw myself turn into a bright crystal and clear body. The clear body was 'me', and I was the clear image. I later realized that I was not the crystal body image, but a clear living being! Over time, this clear living being, became even clearer, and the light which surrounded and permeated this clear being grew brighter and brighter! In this state there were no boundaries of being, but a feeling of 'expansiveness', and of being connected with all living things in the world. I felt comfort, love and serenity – a condition that was so beautiful and still!

As I continued meditating, there was more and more clarity. It was as though I was in clear water. I was transparent, and there was brightness within me. I was a clear living being. I started to feel the *Dhammakaya* image that was clear and bright. At the beginning, there was a tiny *Dhammakaya* image at the center of my body, and I later found that I was inside the *Dhammakaya* image as a successive inner body. Later, I found myself disappearing and becoming one with the clarity.

I currently meditate almost every day, and each meditation lasts around 40 minutes. I sit on a chair or my bed. Sometimes while I meditate, I can feel a tremendous flow of loving-kindness within me. When spreading the loving-kindness and good wishes limitlessly to everyone and everywhere, I can feel the warm-heartedness that it creates.



Meditation has helped me find loving-kindness, healing, and peace. The Dhammakaya International Meditation Center is a refuge in times of crisis. For me, being able to experience that life within reminds me of a Christian Bible verse, which says that "the Kingdom of heaven is within you", or, as Luang Phaw Dhammajayo would say, "the Heaven or Nirvana within".

For those among you who are new to the practice of meditation, I would like to encourage you to continue your practice, and not be discouraged. In the beginning, it may be very difficult to quieten your mind, but I assure you that with continued practice, you will experience the wonderful stillness, healing, and vibrant life, which is available to you during meditation. The 'natural-minded' man looks for miracles outside of himself, but the greatest of miracles is 'within' you.

**Ms. Ann Barton (Australia)**



"I gained a new life by practising meditation. Meditation is a refuge for me. I often see the bright golden Buddha image within me; it is a warm-hearted feeling. Happiness from meditation has replaced the loss of my beloved. I can now stand on my own."

In 1988, I lost my beloved daughter, Yve, in an accident. She died at a public hospital in Sydney, Australia. She was disabled and would go to the hospital for short periodic treatments. She lost her life in an accident as she was sitting in a wheelchair and a safety jacket accidentally winded around her neck and strangled her to death. It was a great loss and caused pain and grief to everyone in the family. Yve was a lovely child and was an important member of our family. She was only 7 years old and she passed away suddenly.



It was a period of great crisis in my life. I had to regain my composure and reassure myself, my husband and our three daughters so as not to be overwhelmed by grief. I had sleep problems and had to rely on sedatives, but they made me more nervous. I went to visit a psychiatrist. I felt better during the visit, but felt worse after I left the office. The loss of my daughter and the grief weighed on me constantly. I tried to talk to my close friends but nothing changed. Sorrow lingered on my mind and in my heart.

Two years later, I was still miserable but I continued to perform my duties as a mother and a wife. I felt like I was a pilot who had to fly a plane to bring the passengers safely to their destination.



In 2001, I took up a position as an English language school teacher in the town of Burwood. I saw a monk in a yellow robe sitting in the waiting room. He smiled at me and I felt delighted. I suddenly felt happy and realised that he could be a spiritual guide for me. The Venerable One was the abbot of the Dhammakaya International Society of Australia in Sydney. He asked if I would teach him how to speak English. I offered to teach without any charges in exchange for meditation lessons. He kindly agreed.

Last year, I encountered a big problem because my husband suddenly decided that he wanted us to go our separate ways. I felt unbelievably stressed. We had been together for 16 years and had gone through difficult times together, including the loss of our daughter, Yve. In the end, he left without any explanation.

On the day that he left, I felt hopeless and depressed. I felt ill and begged him to take me to the hospital. I also felt so confused. On the way to the hospital, we had to cross the street. It was night-time and the traffic was quite busy. I suddenly felt so desperate and lost that I thought about committing suicide. At that moment, my mind returned to the centre of my body, as I had been taught. A large *Dhammakaya* image appeared, expanded and covered my body like a giant tree. He looked at me with loving-kindness and said, "Keep your mind, keep your mind", and the voice I heard was from one of the monks who had taught me meditation.



My consciousness returned and I asked my husband to hold my hand while we crossed the road. I recollected that the *Dhammakaya* image had protected me from committing suicide. My subconscious mind said I gained a new life from practising meditation, which The Venerable One kindly taught me. I am indebted to him and I would not have lived if he had refused to teach me. It has been five years since I began meditating. Meditation is a refuge for me. I often see the bright golden *Dhammakaya* image within me; it is a warm-hearted feeling. Happiness from meditation has replaced the loss of my beloved and I can now stand on my own.

I am anxious to study more about Dhamma and understand it thoroughly. I plan to devote myself to helping the meditation society once I reach 70 years old. I hope that everyone can have the experience of seeing the *Dhammakaya* image within, like I do. It is as if my life has been given a second chance.

**Ms. Khamnoi Saengjai (Thailand)**



"When I met with the accident, I lost both my legs and my husband. At that moment, I felt like I had lost everything. It was difficult to accept, but I still had meditation as my refuge. I did not abandon my meditation. Although I cannot meditate on the floor, I can do it on the wheelchair or the bed every single day. My mind is so accustomed to the practice of meditation at all times."

I felt great sorrow when my husband, the main provider of the family, died from a bus accident in the beginning of 2001. I felt that I had lost everything and cried so much that I didn't eat or sleep. I was so stressed, pressured, confused and worried about my future, that I could not see any way out. I was worried about my children, whom I loved the most. To make matters worse, I had also lost both my legs, could not help myself and didn't know how I could take care of my children aged five and six years old. I felt so alone and I did not have enough money to live on.

Besides my husband's sudden death, another unavoidable event that magnified the suffering further in my life was the amputation of both of my legs as a result of the accident. My right leg was removed just above the knee, and the left leg was removed at my thigh. It was an extremely severe loss —physically and mentally. These days I have to rely on a wheelchair at all times. I have to help myself, but it is awkward and pitiful. Unable to use the artificial legs as they pinched my skin and caused terrible pain and bleeding, I decided to use the wheelchair instead.



After leaving the hospital and recovering at home for 10 days, I had to start learning to help myself because there was just me and my two young children left. I trained and forced my body to do many things, but I was still experiencing terrible pain. The flesh wounds and the area where the bone was still broken had not completely healed yet. I shouldn't have moved around so much, but I had no choice.

From the moment I woke up until I went to bed, I spent most of my time in the wheelchair. In the beginning, I had to teach myself to get onto the wheelchair by myself, because I was on my own and there was no one else to help. I couldn't drink water when I wanted to because it was too high for me to reach. I couldn't eat rice from the cooker because the cooker was also out of my reach. I had no other solution but to climb. Sometimes, I climbed onto the wheelchair, but still I could not reach high enough and would fall off. Blood was everywhere because my wounds were still fresh from surgery. The stitches had not completely closed yet, so the wound reopened. I had to do everything by myself because I did not have anyone else. And of course, I still had my two children to take care of.

I was a legless single mother of two young children at that point of time in my life. I had to take care of my children on top of the challenges I faced when taking care of myself. I had to scoop water to bathe myself and my children and I also had to do the household chores. I endured this for over six months until my wounds healed and there wasn't any bleeding when I forced my body to move. I had to do a heavy load of chores like cooking and laundry, and I had to sell groceries in a rental space which provided a mere income to support my two children. My earnings were only 100-200 baht (US$5) per day. I had to ask the customers to scoop and weigh the rice themselves, but everyone was eager and willing to help. If there was a male customer, I would ask him to pull the sacks of rice out for me. I sat on the wheelchair all day long and I did not have the time to lie down or rest because I had to sit and watch over the store. I was very tired and exhausted. My body was tired and worn because I had to carry out repeated activities. I felt pain at the point where my legs were amputated and was in pain for weeks. It was difficult to describe just how miserable the pain actually was. It was so unbearable that the suffering could not be relieved by any medication.



I went through a lot of grief and suffered every day. Then, I started to watch the DMC programme through a satellite channel and I started to meditate continuously at my home in the Mae Sai district, Chiang Rai province. I suffered for more than a year, but these days I am much happier. I understand more about life through the Law of Kamma that Luang Phaw Dhammajayo teaches. This has helped me to accept the way things are. I've never forgotten to chant and meditate.

I realised that I have to seek the best path of survival for my life. In the beginning, when I practised chanting daily, I had to climb 40 steps to get to the second floor of the house. I had to practise going up the stairs two to three steps at a time. I tried from different angles until I was able to climb all 40 steps. During the first seven to eight days, I felt soreness and pain throughout my entire body, but I never gave up. All I knew was that I had to reach the top and overcome the obstacles by focusing only on the destination.



Later, I asked someone to help move the Buddha stand to a loft which required me to climb up only 20 steps. Despite my condition, I went upstairs to chant and meditate everyday in the mornings and evenings, and have not missed a single day since.

I am preparing myself for inevitable death and I believe we cannot lead our lives carelessly. I intend to fully accumulate all the merits from donating, observing the precepts and meditating. I feel that meditation is the only path that can lead you directly to Nirvana. In addition, meditation makes me very happy.



Whenever I can meditate for a long period, I can see a very clear *Dhammakaya* image. He expands outwards without any boundary. Before going to bed, I meditate and contemplate my merit while visualising a *Dhammakaya* image until I fall asleep. I always try to remind myself that I need to use the remaining of my life to accumulate as much merit as I can. Even though there are days when I am very tired, I will never neglect my meditation. I always thought, "Why should I be lazy? I have so little time on Earth. I have to seek Dhamma for myself. I believe nobody else can help us, therefore we must help ourselves."



Before coming to Wat Phra Dhammakaya, I had already practised meditation. My husband would play a guided meditation tape by Luang Phaw Dhammajayo and I would meditate according to his instructions. I saw a crystal sphere that was clear and bright in my abdomen. At that time, I did not know what it was because I had never meditated before. Later, I saw a picture of a crystal sphere on the cover at the back of a book. I recognised that it was what I had seen, but mine was clearer and a lot brighter. Later in my meditation, I saw many more crystal spheres appearing continuously. My mind felt comfortable. I felt happiness beyond description. Since then, I had never missed a day of meditation. Then one day, I was able to visit the temple.

My meditation experience continued to improve. It was very crisp, clear and bright. When I met with the accident, I lost both my legs and my husband. At that moment, I felt like I had lost everything. It was difficult to accept, but I still had meditation as my refuge. I did not abandon my meditation. Although I cannot meditate on the floor, I can do it on the wheelchair or the bed every single day. My mind is so accustomed to the practice of meditation at all times. Then one day, when my mind was at a standstill, a *Dhammakaya* image appeared. It looked clearer than if I were to see it with my naked eyes. It was crystal clear and very bright. I felt delighted, joyful and happy. I always think that the *Dhammakaya* is the best refuge for me.



When I wake up early at 4 am every morning, the first thing I do is to place my mind lightly at the centre of my body and meditate. After that, I take a shower. Then I go upstairs to chant in the meditation room. I need to climb up 20 steps. Getting upstairs requires a lot of determination and hard work because I don't have legs like other people. I have to use a lot of arm strength and I cannot do it at full strength because my right collarbone was also broken. Even though my left arm was broken into two, I still try to climb up because I want to continue to accumulate merit.



I suffered and felt pain when climbing each step of the stairs. Even though it was extremely difficult, I received enormous bliss in return. After the accident, I didn't have the chance to visit the temple again because I had to look after the store and take care of the children and myself. Going to the temple was not convenient either, but my thoughts were always of the temple. I sent donations to make every merit with Luang Phaw Dhammajayo and have never missed a single merit.

I love the inner crystal body because it is the only thing that makes my heart calm and warm. I think of it all the time and not think of other useless things. I receive the willpower from Luang Phaw Dhammajayo everyday through the DMC programme, which I can apply directly to myself. The customers sometimes ask why my house is so radiant. Some people notice that I have only one channel on and ask what channel it is. I answered by saying, "The DMC channel", and I tell them that there are new stories every day. It makes the other people want to get a satellite dish like mine. Some people wonder how I can maintain my smile and live a difficult life with my condition. I tell them the reason that I've survived till today is because of the inspiring DMC programme that I watch daily and also because I have attained the inner *Dhammakaya*.

Sometimes I would be a *kalyanamitta* or virtuous fellow to others who have suffered also. There was a customer who came to the store regularly. He had family problems and wanted to commit suicide. He already had a chain hung up in his house. When he felt depressed, he put his head through the loop. Once his awareness returned, he wondered, "She has an even more difficult life than mine. With only a minor life problem, why don't I fight it?" Thus, he stopped thinking about suicide and removed his head from the loop. I shared Luang Phaw Dhammajayo's teachings with him. I taught him that human life is valuable and that he should never think about suicide. I talked to him about Dhamma and urged him to make merit and to meditate. Now, he understands better.

The most important thing for me is that I've found the true refuge in my life which is also the real objective of being born human – attaining the *Dhammakaya* within. Otherwise, I might not have had the willpower to continue living.

# Chapter 6

# Wisdom

"A person who earnestly meditates and attains the Dhammakaya will discover that wisdom lies within. When we meditate, a bright light will emerge. We will be able to see this inner light as clear as daylight yet its glow is gentler and more sublime. If we keep seeing this inner light, we will uncover its origin which resembles a crystal ball, much like the sun in the sky which is the source of the golden brightness in the world."

**Luang Phaw Dhammajayo**

## *Pure Inner Wisdom*

Many people have informed me that after they have practised meditation, their daily behaviours and abilities to resolve problems improve significantly. Those who have not experienced meditation might wonder how this is possible. **People who shared their experience with me all agree that, even though they haven't been practising meditation for very long, they can feel that they are calmer and more tranquil. Those who have ugly tempers find themselves more patient. Some say that their minds are more alert. They are able to organise their thinking in a much better way, are more articulate and feel more self-assured. Moreover, they become more creative and decisive. These qualities benefitted their careers greatly.** All of them feel that their thoughts and speech originate from a pure and powerful source.

A person who earnestly meditates and attains the *Dhammakaya* will discover that wisdom lies within. When we meditate, a bright light will emerge. We will be able to see this inner light as clear as daylight, yet its glow is gentler and more sublime. If we keep seeing this inner light, we will uncover its origin which resembles a crystal ball, much like the sun in the sky which is the source of the golden brightness in the world.

With attainment of the *Dhammakaya* through meditation, follows the desire to find the inner wisdom which is the secret of life. The study of inner wisdom will never be associated with loneliness and sorrow. Rather, it is a search for true and lasting joy. The *Dhammakaya* will reveal all secrets and leave us without doubts. We will possess the right knowledge about the purpose of life and consequently follow a correct path - one that is more fruitful and substantive.

## *Living Library*



**Knowledge that we discover through the attainment of the *Dhammakaya* makes us happier and become more well-adjusted individuals. Having true knowledge, which actually lies within ourselves, is so crucial to leading purposeful and meaningful lives. With the *Dhammakaya,* we are like living, breathing libraries, sources of infinite wisdom, purity, happiness and power.** Unlock that knowledge through meditation. This is not difficult to do at all if only we give ourselves a chance.

It is interesting to read the stories of people who practised meditation and discovered that it has helped them solve various difficulties in their lives. Not only have they found home and professional lives more enjoyable, they have also realised the fundamental purpose of their lives on this earth.

Mr. Leon Bourne (United Kingdom)



"I have noticed some side effects from meditation. I used to drink heavily, now I don't. I used to take drugs and smoke, now I don't. I used to be prone to anger, now I am not. My life used to be full of stress and problems, now I deal with those problems and keep stress to a minimum."

I have always known that our physical presence, as we know it, is not all there is to life. I lost my father when I was eight years old. This was my first experience with death and it affected me very deeply. I had a strong feeling that this was not the end of our existence and spent the following years of my life questioning the point of existence on this Earth if life was meant to last for such a short period of time.



When I was in my 20s, I realised that there were too many questions left unanswered by the religions that I had been brought up with. I had developed some extremely bad habits by this time - drinking, smoking and taking pretty much any drugs that I could lay my hands on. Somehow though, through my life's mess, a friend introduced me to meditation known at that time as New Age awareness.

Almost immediately, I started to see benefits in my life in ways that I least expected. The first thing that surprised me was that although I was using meditation tapes that lasted for only half an hour, my meditations seemed to go on a great deal longer and took about two to three hours. It was as if time changed when I was in a meditative state. I also discovered that if I had any questions and asked it to myself as if I were another person during meditation, I would always find the correct answer. Sometimes the correct answer would come after the initial meditation, during my day-to-day life. This made my decision-making better and soon I started to get benefits and improved my social and work life. I gave up smoking, cut down on drinking and almost stopped taking drugs. I went to work in Germany for better income.

A few years before I went to Germany, I had what I call my first life-changing experience through meditation and it blew me away! I was meditating almost daily at this time and on three separate occasions, I felt the need to stop my meditations before I considered them to be complete. This was because I kept coming to a very deep state and felt that if I were to go on, I could not control what would happen. On each of these three occasions, I reached this same point in my meditation more quickly. And eventually I decided to step off the cliff, (which was what it felt like), and went where my meditation took me.

I could still clearly remember what happened that day, 17 years ago, as if it were yesterday. When I started my meditation I quickly reached the edge of the cliff state, and I had to admit that I was very wary of taking that next step. What happened was the hardest thing imaginable to put it in words. I felt like I had stepped off my imaginary cliff, but instead of falling, I was swept away at an unimaginable speed. I was surrounded completely by white spiralling light that moved like the wind in a tornado. I felt fear and excitement, almost like as if electricity was coming from the centre of my body. This beautiful white light carried me to a place that was equally hard to explain. It was like an enormous circle of white light and this time the light was different. It was not swirling with energy but was radiant and glowing like a mist over a pond. I felt like I was floating on air and I had a feeling of immense peace and joy. I could see myself as a beautiful white spirit and other similar looking spirits came to greet me. What surprised me was that I appeared to have a familiarity with those spirits - we communicated without words but with feelings. This was a strange but absolutely unforgettable experience. I stayed as long as I could in this place but I had to go back because I was not sure if I had died. This sounds weird, doesn't it? Nevertheless, the place I 'visited' made me feel at home.

I was so amazed by this experience that I recorded this significant event and carried the piece of paper with me all the time for about four to five years. Unfortunately, my wallet was stolen together with that piece of paper entitled, 'The Day I Danced with Angels'.

I continued to meditate at this time and although I had a number of wonderful experiences, I gradually found myself making less time for my meditations until they faded out. What I did not realise was that my old habits started to wean their way back into my life. The following years became some of the hardest times of my life.

I had taken on a great deal of work and had stopped guiding my decisions with my meditations. Eventually the inevitable happened, one of the companies I worked for forced me into bankruptcy due to owing me a large amount of money. As I had always worked very hard and to a very high standard, I felt that I did not deserve this. My solicitors attempted to take legal action against the company but my money ran out before I could even conclude the case. In the end, I was left a penniless bankrupt. I started drinking and smoking heavily again. Soon, stress and depression returned.

One thing that I was very proud of myself was the fact that I never had problems getting work. When I completed school, I took a job as a carpenter and joiner, and completed a full apprenticeship. I had never been out of work and had never found the need to advertise, as my work was mainly recommended to others by good referrals. Not only did I work on carpentry and joinery now, I worked on newly built houses and extensions and refurbishments of old buildings as well. I enjoyed my work and when things were low, my work kept me going and held me together. In a holistic way, my work led me to meditation again and I considered this to be the most fortunate thing that happened in my life.

In July 2005, it was my luck to be introduced to Phibul Chompolpaisal, who was the secretary of the Dhammakaya International Society of United Kingdom (DISUK). He informed me that my services as a builder could be useful in the conversion of the Brookwood Chapel into a Meditation Centre. So, I offered my services and started work. My work involved staying on the grounds for five days a week. I found the Thai Buddhist way of life becoming very attractive to me during this time. I also felt drawn to find out more about Buddhism and meditation. I now regularly enjoy taking part in the ceremonies and meditation has become part of my everyday life.



I am learning about meditation every day at the *Dhammakaya* meditation society in Woking. I have already stopped smoking and drinking with ease. I have learned about the five precepts and now live by these extremely sensible guidelines. I am using my meditations to make decisions and come to correct conclusions. I have come to understand the importance of merit and in 2006,

I have pledged 10 gold Buddha statues to the Maha Dhammakaya Cetiya in Thailand.

Since meditating the *Dhammakaya* way through visualising a crystal ball, I have had two exceptional meditations. The first was when I spoke about meditation to a Centre volunteer, Hui. She has become my true friend. When I was talking to her one evening after work, we got into a conversation about meditation and she suggested that I should try and bring my mind to the centre of the crystal ball and to keep doing so once I visualise the crystal ball during my meditation. The following evening, I attempted to follow Hui's instructions. I visualised and focused my mind on the crystal ball (which always appears to me with a white glow from the centre). I found that I could relatively easily centre my focus on the very centre and draw myself into the crystal ball. Each time I would spend a moment in the crystal ball and then visualise another crystal ball at its centre and draw my mind into the centre of that; this went on four or five times, each time taking my meditation into a much deeper level. I then found myself in the centre of a beautiful clear crystal with a central core of pure white and coloured petals radiating out from the central core.



The feeling that I had was of electrical energy and immense happiness. I became excited over what I was experiencing and was pulled away from that place. My excitement had caused me to lose focus. It had since become clearer to me that the patterns that many of the *Dhammakaya* members wore on their shirts representing the Dhamma were very similar to what I saw that night. No drawn or painted masterpiece could come anywhere close to the beauty of what I saw. Since then, I tried hard to repeat that experience many times, but unfortunately sometimes trying too hard did not yield results.

I often meditate to help with insomnia. I find that it is an excellent way to stop all the thoughts that keep spinning around in my head. My most recent experience occurred shortly after midnight whereby I had a lot of things on my mind. I knew that if I did not meditate, my head would be spinning all night. So, I sat in the half-lotus position and proceeded to go relax my eyes, nose and so on until I was focused on the centre of the crystal ball. I tried not to do anything.

I gradually became aware of the similar state of being surrounded by light like my first experience years ago. There were many spirits or beings present all around me and my form became clear as crystal. The crystal at the centre of my form became radiant white and glowed. I felt energised and cleansed again. I became aware that my own form was floating inside the form of a giant crystal body and we were sharing the same crystal ball at our cores. I spent some time in this place and as soon as I came out of my meditation I woke my wife up and told her about what had happened excitedly.



I don't know if my meditations could be interpreted or not, but I just know that when I had these experiences, they blew me away! I should say that I have noticed some side effects from meditation. I used to drink heavily, now I don't. I used to take drugs and smoke, now I don't. I used to be prone to anger, now I am not. My life used to be full of stress and problems, now I deal with those problems and keep stress to a minimum level. I have true good friends, a beautiful wife and a wonderful son. My life has become complete and I am contented.

Before I met the wonderful people at the Meditation Centre, I firmly feel that my core belief was peace and this was instilled in me way before my birth. When my father passed away I had an unbelievably strong feeling that his death was not the end. The fact that I discovered meditation on my own accord and had such deep experiences all those years ago was a prelude to what has happened now in my life. It has been the greatest honour to become involved with the *Dhammakaya* meditation society, and my fondest wish is to continue to do so. My past was built here and my future will forever be with meditation.

**Dr. JoAnn Borda Sainz, Ph.D (U.S.A.)**



"I want to share the fact that *Dhammakaya* meditation offers a quick and non-complicated vehicle to pursue inner happiness and peace and a change of outlook on life and mankind, an outlook of hope and peace."

We are a composite of our experiences. My life was shaped as the youngest child of Latin American immigrants from Colombia, South America. As I follow life's path, I have grown and developed and I have had many spiritual awakenings. When I am ready, things start to "click" and make sense. This is what happened when I arrived at the Dhammakaya International Meditation Center (DIMC) in Fanwood, New Jersey in 2005.



Though I had chanted and practiced meditation at different times since 1974, its deep meaning did not crystallize for me until I attended the DIMC. I began to study a "process and system" that was fully accessible and comprehensible, and this developed as I experienced life.

Prior to 2005, my religious and spiritual experiences provided only pieces of a puzzle to my understanding of life's spirituality. I had begun my religious studies as a six year old, and later chanted. I was exposed to many different forms of meditation, prayers, many religions, sects and many languages Hinduism, Buddhism, Quakerism, Roman Catholicism, Protestantism, mysticism, Brazilian Candomble Hindu, Chinese, Japanese, Korean and Spanish. Now, here I am, in 2005, learning Pali, in yet another quest for the Divine, through the *Dhammakaya*.



When I attended my first session at the DIMC, my husband had recently passed away. We had been married for 38 years and I never imagined that I would survive without him because I was so dependent on him.

I have been an educator since 1968, and have taught, supervised, and administered programs from elementary to Ph.D. levels. I am currently an Assistant Principal at the same school where I once served as a Spanish teacher, but now it is a multi-school campus, an "oasis" in a high crime, depressed area, where 'crack' was invented.



DIMC for me has represented an encounter with love, beginning with the abbot, and permeating every aspect of the Center: the attending monks, staffs, the educator, other assistants and teachers, an impeccable setting, providing a haven for surrounding communities through classes, chanting, meditation, retreats, courses, and other social events. We are all made to feel like pure and innocent children on a quest, through the guidance of each and every staff member.

The degree of patience for where we are in our spiritual journey is quite remarkable. I have learned that we can work miracles by realizing the miracle within ourselves. To transform the world we must first transform ourselves and realize that we belong to one great spiritual family, the world. Everything we do, whether good or evil, affects the world cosmically. In the level of spirit, we are all one.



Among the concepts I have internalized from the DIMC are the followings:

1) **Approach meditation with a positive heart**, otherwise, your meditation will be adversely affected. I remember being frightened and crying during meditation because I had not fully centered my mind. I was distracted, causing an

adverse effect on my meditation. I have since overcomed this problem through greater awareness of the mind and the need to "empty the mind of all worries".

2) **Forgive our shortcomings**. We cannot love others if we do not love ourselves. Since 1999, I have not been able to sit in the Lotus position. Indeed, I will never be able to again do this, since I had a hip replacement, and to do so would be counter-productive in my case. Instead, I have to accept my physical limitations and love myself with what and where I am today.

3) **Practice meditation systematically and regularly.** Meditation enables us to attain

nirvana, *Dhammakaya*, so it is to our advantage that we develop this practice as a habit and ritual. I am working on this area. I have the advantage of working an hour away from home. I listen to chants at least six times a day and am making great progress although I have never formally studied Pali. I get great comfort from chanting, especially the part that addresses Karma: ***yam kammam karissanti***.



4) **Seek the divine light within,** beginning with the crystal starting from within us and extending this light throughout the world: the light of loving kindness that we hope will touch all, even if others have hurt us; when we have done this we become one with the Divine and we gain a merit for ourselves and for our loved ones.

5) **Take this light with you everywhere.** We can replicate the meditative bliss we achieved at the DIMC in every waking moment, and in our every location in a "moving, waking meditation".

6) **Transform the world by first transforming ourselves** and realize that we belong to one great spiritual family - the world; and know that everything we do, whether good or evil, affects our karma. Life is a dynamic process. In the level of spirit, we are all one.

7) **Meditate without resistance.** Acknowledge fleeting thoughts, look at them but without expending judgment, resistance or interest. Revert to chanting **'Samma Arahang'** when becoming

distracted and losing focus and radiate love as if through the "brightness of the sun" and the "serenity of the moon".

8) **Cherish the sense of peace and love as you spread this love throughout the world.** In the past, I have had some frightening meditations, but now I realize it is only because I approached the meditation process with negativity. I realize that I get from meditation what I bring to it, so that it is very important to empty the mind of any thoughts and worries.



I am interested in meditation because it is a vehicle to pursue our inner divinity and connection to humanity. When I practice meditation, I focus the mind by first preparing myself to be positive and empty myself of any negative feelings, whether physical, psychological or emotional in nature so that my meditation experience will not be adversely affected.

First, I adjust my posture, breathe deeply and follow the prescribed path, emptying my thoughts by chanting **'Samma Arahang'**, then patiently sit and wait until I experience the magic of meditation – inner peace, accepting wherever I am and letting everything go past, without resistance or struggle. After experiencing an initial darkness, the focus on a crystal sphere helps restore and rekindle a splendid light, first small and narrow, and then spreading throughout every cell, my entire surroundings, and ultimately the world.

After being guided throughout this process, I sent my loving kindness throughout the world through my inner light, a light of goodness and love that is radiated into the brightness of the sun and the serenity of the moon. The result is one of greater spirituality and connection with my world and a great sense of peace and love for myself and the world.



I think of a clear crystal ball as the object at the center of the body. I use the mantra to keep me centered whenever I feel distracted. Each time the meditation experience is different, depending on what I bring into the meditation.

After meditation, I feel spiritually purified, happy, calm and renewed in hope. I know that change is a question of habit. If we feel such bliss, we should repeat the process often and regularly. Meditation requires discipline, repetition and willpower, so that we do not regress or lose what we have gained. Others know that I meditate. My principal from another faculty and students say, "Why are you always happy? Why don't you get angry? Why don't you curse? How come you love everyone? How come you are so cool and never let anything bother you, no matter what?" I want to share the fact that *Dhammakaya* meditation offers a quick and non-complicated vehicle to pursue inner happiness and peace. You will also experience a change of outlook on life and mankind and an outlook of hope and peace. I often talk to the toughest students and tell them that I am praying for them. One of them replied, "I am praying for you." And I have responded, "This is the greatest gift you could give me, because prayers from a child are even more sacred and regarded." These are youths who are instilled with hope despite being pressed by wounds of society.

I think the fact that my mind is open to considering new ideas is a positive asset to my work. By pointing out to students how to balance thoughts, relations with truth, that through my enriched background, I will be better able to help students turn their lives around. There is always the hope that they will change negative actions toward society to positive interactions and create a more loving world.

People make decisions based on the way I act, my attitude and my acceptance of them as rational beings. If we want to change society, we must start early by instilling the right values in elementary school. Thus, when children become adults, they will be more caring, more loving, and more aware that the world is really one large family that is connected, so that whatever we do on a personal level affects the grand level. This is the first time that I have grasped the concept of replicating the energies in meditation in everyday life.

Mr. Chan Poi Koun (Singapore)



"Once I started meditating, my life began to change. I am more calm and not as serious as I was before. I feel I can release my anxiety, but most importantly, I now see things at a much deeper level. Whatever we see in meditation, we see with our minds, not with the physical eyes."

My name is Chan Poi Koun (Ken), a single Singaporean. I'm 40 years old. I worked as a product manager for a multinational electronic components distribution company in Singapore. I had enjoyed a comfortable life in Singapore. In general, this is what a bachelor in Singapore would hope to gain during the life of his career after graduating from an educational institute.

Less than six years ago, I accidentally met an old classmate in a tennis session. He invited me to learn *Dhammakaya* meditation. I agreed as I wished to find a way to relax my mind. Now I practise meditation daily and accumulate 'merit' at the temple.

As I started meditation practice about three to four years ago, I obtained a certain level of inner meditation experience. I began meditating without having any thoughts or using any mantras. This allowed me to fully relax. I simply placed my mind at the centre of my body. When I did this regularly, I became accustomed to it. Presently, I am able to place my mind in the centre within five minutes.



After that, the feeling of my hands, arms, legs, body, chest, stomach, and the rest of the body seems to disappear. I feel only my heart beating gently. My heart rate, almost at zero, made me feel that my body disappeared, but I am still alive. At that time, I felt that all feelings were gone except for the thought that, "I was within myself."

After that, I saw a crystal ball; the first one was the size of an egg yolk appearing in the centre of my body. Its brightness was that of a full moon.

This brightness didn't hurt my eyes. I compared the crystal ball to a yolk because I couldn't think of anything else that was similar to what I saw.

I continued focusing at it peacefully, when four more crystal balls of the same size and brightness as the initial one appeared. All five spheres combined into one sphere in the center of my body. I felt really good and more relaxed. After that, many more bright and shiny spheres appeared numerous times at the centre of my body. I simply observed them. They happened automatically without any thoughts at all.

I recognised the difference between "thinking", which required energy during a process, compared to "non-thinking", which happened while meditating when no effort was utilised at all.

I didn't want to come out of this comfort zone. I wanted to continue sitting and observing. I didn't feel tired, cold or hot, or uncomfortable, and I felt I could sit in that position for hours. I felt so much happiness that I couldn't put it into words. This is happiness unlike any other, which I'm certain I won't be able to find elsewhere. Now, even with my eyes open, I can still maintain that state at all times.



Once I started meditating, my life began to change. I am more calm and not as serious as I was before. I feel I can release my anxiety, but most importantly, I now see things at a much deeper level. Whatever we see in meditation, we see with our minds, not the physical eyes.

I began to understand that I can't obtain truth or 'happiness' from the external material world. I even try to verify it myself in my career life. The endless pursuit of higher positions on my own career path will only lead me to an endless round of greater responsibility and more complex issues. And it would only get worse rather than better, in terms of losing control of my true self. Money accumulated in bank accounts will eventually just become a game of 'numbers'.



I also feel that I look at things around me in a totally different way. By using our own 'physical eyes' to look at things happening around us, we are sometimes deceived and led away from the truth. For example, what is the true 'happiness' that I really need? I now know that happiness gained from the external material world will not last long and will create more desire, and then we will ask for more. If we live within our means in a basic lifestyle, we can help reduce our desire level. At that point, we would realise that we can survive very well with these basic needs and the happiness of 'no desire' is the lasting one.

I also began to pay attention to matters that previously appeared to be mysterious to me or that I hadn't even thought about and, in doing so, much of what I had not understood became as clear as a pool of clean water. For example, what are we as human beings born for? Is it that we are just raised by our parents, start receiving education, then work, marry, have children, become old and pass away? What is the true meaning of being born as a human in this world?



I'm quite sure many of us have never thought about this question in depth before. As if it is not even a question or an issue at all. If you try to answer this question yourself, you will start to realise that perhaps some of our actions appear unwise in the long term aspect of our lives. We are born with nothing and when we are dead we also cannot bring anything along (and this certainly includes our houses and the money we strived so hard to earn in our lives). Eventually, no matter how successful you are, the end result is still the same: "Ashes to ashes, dust to dust."

I also discovered that there were certain work-related issues that were bothering me. During the morning meditation session, the "solutions" to those issues appeared in my mind automatically without me searching for them. I began to realise that I had those solutions with me all the while.

All that I am speaking of are the results after I started to practise meditation. These are the benefits that I gained, since practising *Dhammakaya* meditation. For me, the practice of meditation allowed me to gain both happiness and wisdom simultaneously.

The happiness is the totally borderless feeling during meditation: the type of happiness which is present during a totally relaxed and calm state. Once you practise sitting in the cross-legged position, you will get it every time. Success in meditation doesn't depend on any external factors, but simply on your willingness to sit down to meditate.

The wisdom I search for in my life is to understand the true meaning of happiness. It is this meditation which helps to unlock the unlimited inner wisdom within ourselves. It far surpasses the results you would get from simply reading or studying. And this knowledge will uplift your mental quality to a high level, not just solve your current issues, but aid you in your future decisions. You will find that you already have a person of great wisdom within you.



I believe that whoever practises *Dhammakaya* meditation will have similar positive experiences and results as I had.

**Venerable Paul Silasangvaro (U.S.A.)**



"I have learned to respect and to understand people with different perspectives. My relationship with my co-workers has improved tremendously. I have used meditation, as a manager, to resolve problems at work. I found that if I took the time to refresh my mind, I would spend less time fixing things and I would work more effectively. Instead of eating or shopping to forget about

**problems, as I used to do, I now meditate to relax and to find more creative ways to resolve problems."**

My name is Paul Silasangvaro (Pentecost). I am 62 years old and I live in America.



Eight years ago, a friend invited me to attend a meditation program in Azusa, California. There were 10 meditation classes in this program. I decided to join the program, because I wanted to find ways to relieve work-related stress.

I thought that a meditation practice would not be harmful. If I did not like meditation, I could stop at any time. I diligently practiced meditation, to reduce stress, without any intention to see or to know anything. Before trying the Dhammakaya Technique, I had tried other methods of meditation that did not seem to work. I really wanted to try the Dhammakaya Meditation Technique.

In the beginning, I experienced many difficulties. At first, I could not sit in the lotus position for a long time. I needed to sit in a chair to feel comfortable. My mind wandered all the time. When I tried to keep it still, it was like trying to get a monkey to sit still. At times, I was able to keep my mind still for a few minutes. Even then, a short period gave me the feeling of inner peace and enough motivation to continue meditating. I went to the meditation class every Tuesday night and carefully followed the guidance of the instructing monk. I felt a little bit more peaceful with each meditation. I was eventually able to see the crystal ball, although initially not clearly.

I meditated, at home and at work, to relax and relieve stress. I never thought of gaining or seeing anything. I just wanted to continue meditating until my mind was pure. At about the sixth week, all the students in class had to blow bubbles through holders shaped like a crescent moon, a star, and a triangle. No matter what the holder shape was, the bubbles always came out round. We meditated after we blew bubbles and I remembered the image of the bubbles floating in the air clearly.

I closed my eyes slightly and quietly thought of the bubbles. I was trying to keep my mind at the center of my body. After a short while, my mind became still and the image of the bubbles was gone. Something like a crystal ball appeared in place of the bubble at the center of my body. The crystal ball looked bright and shiny. It was much more beautiful than the bubbles I had been imagining. I was able to mentally see the crystal ball from every angle! I found that our physical eyes could see things from only one angle. Our mental eye can see things from every angle, so it can provide a more accurate perspective on things. I felt happy and surprised. I had never thought of seeing a crystal ball within myself. I became excited and this interrupted my mind causing the crystal ball to disappear. I still felt the calmness and peace for many hours afterwards.



With four years of meditation experience, I saw the crystal ball becoming more steady. I was able to stop my thoughts easily when meditate. I found that when I wanted to stop thinking, I was able to stop thinking.

Sometimes, I would see a chain of crystal balls coming from the center of my body. Each sphere provided warmth, safety and peace. If I kept my mind focused on each crystal ball, I could feel the happiness increasing in my body. It was as if an invisible "happiness cloak" had been placed over me. Each new crystal ball gave a sense of more happiness than the previous one. I felt an ecstasy that I never thought possible in meditation, a true happiness like nothing else.



From those experiences, I was inspired to meditate more often. One day while I was meditating, I saw myself appearing in the crystal ball. At that moment, I felt my body become one with the air and a warm ray blanketed my entire body. I saw a beautiful crystal ball shining. Once inside the crystal, I felt myself looking at my own image. It was as clear as the crystal. I was shocked, but I could not deny that I felt very happy. It was as if I was bathing in a river of happiness. The body within looked alive, perfect, and more beautiful than anyone or anything I had ever seen in my life. A deep feeling of calmness spread throughout my body, from the center of my body to the tips of my fingers. It was such a wonderful feeling, that was beyond description.

Although I felt wonderful, I was still surprised to see the body within myself. I never knew that such a thing existed. I asked the instructing monk many questions about this crystal body. I told him I felt happy but wasn't sure of the body I saw inside. He assured me that seeing the body within was a natural phenomenon. I did not need to change my religion. He told me that I had seen the *Dhammakaya*, the refined body of knowing Dhamma on my own. Anyone who keeps his or her mind still will see the same thing, just like when we see the same moon or sun. The *Dhammakaya* is a natural part of every human, like our mind. The *Dhammakaya* has been there, naturally, since we were born. The *Dhammakaya* has nothing to do with religion, race, or personal belief. Just because I cannot see the *Dhammakaya* with my physical eyes, does not mean that there is no *Dhammakaya*. He also added, the *Dhammakaya* body is my own refined self and I need to refine my mind to be able to see it.



We talked for about four hours. The instructing monk explained the true nature of human beings, explaining knowledge which scientists have been unable to discover. He had never discussed the refined body before. Therefore, I did not have any expectations of seeing it. He wanted me to discover the refined body on my own, without external influence by anyone or anything.

Despite his reasonable explanation, deep inside I refused to acknowledge the existence of the *Dhammakaya*. I was actually so agitated that I stopped meditating for two months. Still, I could not stop thinking about the great feelings that came from the center of my body. I decided to begin meditating again, but this time I only wanted to see the crystal ball.



I was able to see the crystal ball again not long afterwards. Two years later, I saw the *Dhammakaya* body again. My personal meditation experience has confirmed that the *Dhammakaya* exists. I have slowly accepted the existence of the *Dhammakaya* body as an integral part of myself. The *Dhammakaya* body is the true source of all happiness.

As I continued to practice meditation, I could clearly see that the *Dhammakaya* body was a refined body within me, purer and wiser than my physical self was. Seeing the *Dhammakaya* body makes me feel calm, peaceful and happy, like nothing else. It is happiness beyond what anyone or anything can imagine.

When I meditate and see the *Dhammakaya* in the center of my body, time seems to go by quickly. An hour seems to pass as quickly as 10 minutes. I began to meditate from two hours to four hours per day, even as I continued to work as a full-time division manager. Since I began the practice of meditation, my lifestyle has become more simple, smooth and peaceful. I do not get irritated like I used to, and I have become more tolerant, to certain behaviors of other people.

I feel less anxious and stressed. I have learned to think from my center, instead of using only my mind. I started to use my mind, when dealing with my colleagues, instead of my external eyes, because our physical eyes do not allow us to see the true reality of things. Our external eyes may also be biased.



I have learned to respect and to understand people with different perspectives. My relationship with my co-workers improved tremendously. I used meditation, as a manager, to resolve problems at work. I found that if I took the time to refresh my mind, I would spend less time fixing things and I would work more effectively. Instead of eating or shopping to forget about problems, as I used to do, I now meditate to relax and to find more creative ways to resolve problems.

One day, I came to the realization that most people are continually searching for new and current things to bring themselves happiness.

Even after they have obtained these things, they are still unhappy. Therefore, they start searching for other things or other people that can give them happiness. It is as if they are chasing after happiness. When they are near happiness, it disappears. Now I believe that I cannot chase after true happiness or purchase it. I find happiness at my center, in meditation. Happiness comes when the mind is still or when I perform good deeds for others. Finally, I decided to enter Buddhist monkhood.



I have come to believe that everyone, irrespective of their educational background, wealth or financial situation - deserves to be as happy as they can be. I have come to believe that everyone needs to have knowledge of the *Dhammakaya* in order to reach true happiness.

# *Chapter 7*

# Peace

"Once our serene spirit is fulfilled with awareness and wisdom, infinite happiness and peace will follow. World peace comes from within, and the origin of peace starts from focusing the mind."

**Luang Phaw Dhammajayo**

## The Origin of World Peace

Everyone wishes to live in a world of peace and happiness. Peace is very precious to all human beings. However, through our inability to accept our differences in race, religion, heritage, tradition and beliefs, we destroy what we most value.



Even though it sounds incredible, all conflicts can be resolved through meditation. When all of us can successfully practise meditation, we will attain the same thing – *Dhammakaya*, which is the source of happiness, purity and enlightenment. Then, the conflicts in our minds will be dissolved. We will recognise that all humanity is composed of family and friends. With the *Dhammakaya*, being kind, caring, and generous comes easily and naturally, and we will lead fulfilling lives. Only positive emotions remain and radiate from us to those around us - our close friends, neighbourhoods, communities, countries and eventually to the entire world. Happiness begins from this tiny point, the centre of your body. When your mind is at rest there, no bad thoughts or feelings may enter you. Inner peace will spread like a fresh breeze from the mountains. The most important goal you can accomplish in life is to attain that peace.



## *Similarities in the Differences*

Achieving inner happiness is necessary in order to create peace for yourself as an individual, for your country and for the world. Once achieved, differences which used to divide us become insignificant, and the similarities become undeniably apparent. Despite the external differences in nationality, heredity, appearance, livelihood, and so on, internally, the inner peace and happiness we feel is identical. Awareness will replace confusion and misunderstanding. The corruption of the environment and human life will be terminated when we all reach the *Dhammakaya*. True peace and tranquility will be a reality for all human beings. Through meditation we learn of the truth of life, the knowledge of which encourages love and goodwill to bloom in the minds of people who possess it. The happiness and peace dreamed about by generations before us, will become real.



The world needs people who pursue inner peace. From them, world peace will be more than a possibility. They are the starting points of peace and a source of knowledge for others who also wish to learn meditation. They inspire us and are role models for others to follow until everyone in the world attains genuine peace.

The attainment of happiness through meditation is our goal. Simply focus the mind inside the body at the centre. There is nothing else to do than this. Through this simple method, our minds will improve, develop and understand life better. Although this is merely at the initial level, we will feel a hint of the indescribable inner happiness that awaits. We will live to perform virtues and share these virtues with humankind. Then, true happiness will grow and expand throughout the world. It will become the world where all humankind can live in harmony.

I wish for everyone to create peace through meditation because it is effective and does not require many resources. Creating peace is much cheaper than waging wars. Wars waste a lot of money and lives, but peace does not require resources or weapons. We just have to focus our minds to attain the *Dhammakaya* within. But if we do it only on our own, peace will not reach far. We all need to cooperate. One person cannot make it happen nor can several people. Everyone throughout the entire world must make a concerted effort to help.



## Manner of Peace

We should make a sincere effort to make peace happen in this world before we die. We can leave this life happily if we know we have accomplished this. Concentrate the mind at the seventh base at the centre of our body and sit in the position of peace. That means sitting cross-legged with your right leg over your left leg, your right hand over your left hand, your right index finger touching your left thumb on your lap, your body upright, your mind fully conscious and then gently closing your eyes, relaxed and comfortable. When you meditate you are giving positively to the world.

Therefore, the very thing that was unimaginable in this world may suddenly happen in the easiest way. It is very possible and very easy for you to attain inner peace. In fact, many people have learned to do so.

The following personal experiences are stories shared by those who extinguished the flames in their minds, allowing the serene glow of peace to grow and expand. Let us learn from their experiences that nothing can prevent us from inner peace as well as universal peace.

**Reverend Richard Salvatore Esposito**
**Ph. B, LOCM (U.S.A.)**

"Meditation slowly transforms sorrow into happiness and peace! And even as I write this, I have come to understand and experience a real peace of mind and a sustained happiness. That sense of guilt is gone and in its place is peace, a very real peace, a peace "that surpasses conventional wisdom and understanding."

As I look back upon my life and reflect, I readily admit that I have not experienced everything in the world there is to encounter, nor do I pretend to know a fraction of all there is to know and understand about life.

Nevertheless, through the odyssey that has been my sojourn this far, in search of an ultimate purpose, I found "my answers" and I found something else I thought to be unattainable. I have traveled around the world, and down many different paths, which has taken me to my greatest personal discovery and realization.



To a greater or lesser degree, we are all involved in this same universal quest, since time immemorial. Great kings and beggars, the mighty and the feeble, the brilliant and simple-minded, the proud and the humble of heart, all seek peace... genuine peace.

The very Constitution of the United States of America guarantees, "The right to life, liberty and the pursuit of happiness"... but guaranteeing the right to seek happiness does not necessarily produce it. Only inner peace, realized individually through meditation, can create, perpetuate and radiate happiness outward to others.



I am an Italian-American born in New York City, and I am a decorated Vietnam Veteran. I have been a Licensed Ordained Christian minister since 1971, and hold university level degrees in Philosophy, Post-Secondary Education, with Post Graduate studies in Psychology and Respiratory Medicine.

My Christian ministry has taken me on many distant journeys to such far-flung places as Costa Rica, Guatemala, South Africa, Swaziland, Angola and throughout Puerto Rico and the Caribbean Basin as well as many parts of the USA.



I have traveled to South America, to Brazil and worked in its teaming cities reaching out to the abused, lost and forgotten "street children", and to the jungle's edge along the great Amazon River, as a medical missionary, helping the infirmed indigenous natives who live in those remote areas.

I have ministered as an evangelist, educator, pastor, and published author, and served as the Academic Dean of The Caribbean Bible College of Puerto Rico in the 1980s.

It has been my good fortune to have led, thus far, a multi-faceted life, both professionally as a corporate executive, in the medical-technical field, teacher and in a ministerial capacity.

Before my conversion to Christianity, I studied Buddhism extensively, taught by monks in Ubon, Thailand.



I have repeatedly witnessed, from culture to culture, from nation to nation, from creed to creed, all of humankind, from the indigenous peoples living deep in the heart of the Amazon jungle to sophisticated stock brokers on Wall Street. All of these people long for, and seek after, inner peace, peace of mind and lasting happiness of heart.

While speaking to a young physician, we discussed the ultimate goal of any good doctor. I mentioned the axiom I studied that stated, "A good physician always strives to ***treat the cause, not the symptom***". Upon saying that, the young doctor chuckled! When I inquired as to what was so humorous about that time-tested maxim, he promptly told me 'his' motto. As a newly graduated physician of the 21st Century his was something very different. He stated emphatically, ***"Whatever works, is good".***

There is a profound practical wisdom in that saying. What I will share with you herein is based somewhat on this simple premise, ***"Whatever works, is good"…*** which is to say, whatever can promote a permanent cure, a genuine healing, is good!

I first set foot on Thai soil in July 1967. I was a soldier during the Vietnam War, from 1964 to 1968. I enlisted in the military at the age of 17, just one month after graduating from high school.



That final year of my military service in South-East Asia was to change the course of my life forever. I was thrust into that horrific, futile conflict at the height of the war, and was to return home far older than my years, for the pain, suffering and death I witnessed.

I was fortunate never to have taken a life, but I served for a period of time attending to the wounded and saw many of my young comrades maimed and killed. The average age of all the soldiers that served was just 19 years old. We were young and vital, and with the brashness of youth thought ourselves to be invincible... but alas, such was not the case.

It was during that year, while stationed in Thailand, that I came to know and love the Thai people and their rich culture. Their way of life became an oasis of harmony in the midst of the mayhem and discord of war. Their revered King taught his people, "to be content, with enough".

Such was my deep love for this land and its people that it became my life-long aspiration to return to the Kingdom of Thailand and live, and so I have.

The vast majority of Thai people are kind, gentle, truly unassuming and quietly content. They possess a distinct dignity and poise, matched only by their genuine graciousness and enchanting charm! My heart has become inextricably knit to this unique and amazing land of smiles, tranquility and the Buddhist faith that makes it so.

When I arrived in Thailand to live, my very first request was to be taken to a temple. I wanted to pay my respects to the resident monks there, and express my gratitude at finally being able to return to the only place on Earth that I truly felt was home. That temple was Wat Phra Dhammakaya, the Dhammakaya Temple and Foundation, in Pathum Thani Province, Thailand, a place like no other!



It was there, that I was introduced, for the first time in my life, to the art and science of an ancient method of meditation, a technique leading to the attainment of the *Dhammakaya*.

The central theme, primary mission and vision of the Dhammakaya Foundation and Temple, is to instruct in and promote the practice of meditation around the world. Expert, highly trained and experienced Buddhist monks teach meditation there continually, with regularly scheduled programs and retreats for Westerners. These dedicated men have devoted their entire lives to purity. It is a noble and life-changing mission.

And so, I sat for the first time in my life, under the teachings of a Venerable, on the *Dhammakaya* method of meditation and my personal "journey to joy", and a remarkable inner adventure of discovery and change began.

The introductory *Dhammakaya* Meditation technique was explained, and I followed the simple instructions as they were given, step by step, by my teaching monk.

First, closing my eyes gently and relaxing every part of my body, I listened only to the soothing sound of the monk's voice. Following his guiding instructions I became deeply relaxed, my body, tense and tight, became increasingly supple and then … it became light as a feather!



As I began to meditate, concentrating my attention on an imagined fixed object in my mind's eye, I envisioned a bright full moon on which to focus. But I was continually distracted at the torrent of thoughts that surged through my mind non-stop, one after the other, arising and disappearing only to be replaced by another, and then another! I never realized how resistant and restless the churning of my mind actually was until I tried to stop the frantic deluge of thoughts, each vying for my attention!

I realized, then, for the first time in my life, how frenzied my "untrained mind" was after a lifetime of being taught to think, analyze, and reason, from my earliest childhood. Up until that moment in time, I had never attempted to "stop all thought and bring my mind to a complete standstill and to rest" ... which is the absolute essence of the *Dhammakaya* method of meditation.

But like anything else that is to be mastered, meditation takes time and a genuine commitment to practice with a highly trained, experienced teacher. Little did I realize that my first twenty-minute session was to alter the course of my understanding and life, for all time.

When my teaching monk finished his preparatory instructions, we sat in total silence. And as I sat, eyes closed, and still, although we were in a quiet and comfortable room, far from the maddening pace of the city, incredibly, I could still hear the noise from the bustling traffic and incessant activity of Bangkok churning about in my mind! Thoughts began to arise at what seemed to be an uncontrollable pace!



Gradually, the incessant torrent of chaotic thoughts decreased until they subsided to just five or six arising every few minutes, and I was able to experience a few moments of true stillness and serene peace. It was a revelation!

From that fateful day to this, my first foray into the daily practice of the *Dhammakaya* method of meditation has become an invaluable part of my life. And the adage of that young physician that … ***"Whatever works is good",*** took on a special meaning; indeed, **"meditation works"!**

The first profound change in my life, that I can attribute directly to my daily practice of meditation, is the miraculous ability to gradually learn how to, "Let go and begin to live in the present". To let go of the past and learn to live in the moment was something I thought to be utterly impossible, and for good reason!

For decades, I carried within me a deep sense of guilt. A burden that I believed nothing or nobody could lift. During the height of the Vietnam War, during the Tet Offensive, a very close friend of mine insisted on taking my place on a dangerous patrol. I had been exhausted from a 23-day mission trekking through dense jungle.

No sooner had we returned to the base, I was then ordered to go back out with little or no rest. It was then that my friend insisted on taking my place. He insisted and I relented. That very night, he was killed in action, attempting to evacuate the wounded from a Fire Base in An Loc. The carnage of that battle was beyond description, just a handful of young men were left alive, barely.



I was devastated at receiving the news. For years my dreams were filled with images of the wounded and dying, their faces always before me. I became bitter and my heart heavy, and no words of consolation or reason could rationalize away the idea in my mind that, "I was responsible" for my friend's untimely demise. For more than three decades I labored under the weight of this sorrow.

Many people, conditioned and driven by modern materialistic values, seek instant results, instant gratification, instant peace. What I discovered as I practiced the *Dhammakaya* method of meditation, day by day, was a palpable yet subtle change in my mind and heart, barely noticeable at first.



Meditation slowly transforms sorrow into happiness and peace! And even as I write this, I have come to understand and experience a real peace of mind and a sustained happiness. That sense of guilt is gone and in its place is peace, a very real peace, a peace "that surpasses conventional wisdom and understanding". I am free from the shackles of the past and now live in the moment.

**Mr. Farid (Iran)**



"I have now learned that meditation can truly help everyone. People lack a peaceful and happy mind. It is not only people involved in wars who lack a happy and peaceful mind, but also every person in this world."

My name is Farid. I am a 46 year-old Muslim businessman living in Tehran, Iran. I have a terrific wife and a lovely daughter. After reading a book about meditation, I became very interested in it. Later, visitors to Iran showed me how to meditate and introduced me to DMC. I learned how to meditate by placing my mind in the middle of my stomach. I memorised this method and continued meditating at home while my family was asleep because all was quiet.



That night was a great and wonderful night. Closing my eyes gently and comfortably, I thought about relaxing and walking under the moonlight and thought of the moon in the middle of my stomach. A little while later, my body felt as light as a feather, empty, and happy. Inner happiness is totally different from, and tremendously more luxurious than having a Mercedes Benz or a huge mansion. Reaching the moon inside, I felt inner delight. A while later, I saw the moon floating in front of me, and just observed it. After just a moment, it automatically moved into my abdomen.

I thought the head was the important point in meditation. But in reality, I found that the significant point is at the centre of the body. When I discovered the inner brightness and inner bliss from meditation, I realised that I had found the light as opposed to losing myself in darkness in the past.



Extremely glad, joyful and delighted, I knew that meditation was true happiness. Having a big house or an air conditioner is not true happiness. In the past, I was easily irritated. If anyone made noise before bedtime or honked their horn, it would make me angry. But now, I do not have any anger left. I can forgive others. I forgive the mistakes of others and do not take it personally.

I believe that meditation has nothing to do with religion, age, or faith. It is so cosmopolitan that anyone can do it and experience true peace. I organised a meditation course at my home and invited Iranians to meditate. I first asked them these questions, "How are you doing, my friend? Are you exhausted? Are you tired of a monotonous life?" Everyone unanimously answered, "I'm so tired. The more problems I have, the more bored I become. It's all very boring. I'm tired of my boss. I'm tired of everything." So then, I invited them to meditate. They said, "O.K." and came. They also felt that meditation made them much better. It was a very good feeling.

I believe that there is no one in this world who experiences no problems, whether they are from the lower class, the middle class, or the upper class. If we can still our mind for ten or 20 minutes, we will have energy to solve difficult problems. People tend to have the goal in life of only becoming rich, having a beautiful house or having a car. However, when these goals are achieved, they become bored. If everyone's goal is to have a happy mind, they will not become bored and will not want to leave that happiness. They will not want to leave the inner happiness. This explains why people in the upper class or high societies in Iran are very affectionate towards meditation. Meditation is a trend among high societies here. There were 20 people who came to meditate at my home the first time. But in the second session, can you guess how many people showed up? 60 people!

My wife also meditates. With the great desire to meditate, she gets up at 3 a.m. I don't know why it has to be 3 a.m. She automatically gets up at 3 a.m. She says that her mind is clear, light, and comfortable. Being able to focus her mind and following the method easily, she seems to be in an especially good mood. When we organised the meditation course, my daughter, who is only four-and-a-half years old, observed what the adults were doing. Then, she sat next to me and said, "Just sitting still and closing my eyes, I can do that." She sat and closed her eyes. Surprisingly, she could sit for almost ten minutes. Prior to this, she could not be still and was very playful. She pulled her own hair all the time resulting in significant hair loss. Since she began meditating, she has not pulled her hair anymore. She is very calm. I was so glad; I quickly took a picture of her and sent the image via e-mail to my relatives living throughout Iran. I have now learned that meditation can truly help everyone. It is not only people in wars who lack a happy and peaceful mind, but also everyone in this world.

**Mr. Wren Mast-Ingle (South Africa)**



"Through meditation I have been regenerated in mind, body and being. I see things and people as I have never seen them before. The scientific community has defined us as manifestations of vibrations. In fact all physical matter is no more than denser oscillations of cellular activity."

My life is truly amazing. It is filled with a richness of experience in mind, body and being that defies words of explanation.

I started very badly 67 years ago suffering from every conceivable form of illness that continued until fourteen. It was then that I took up Hatha Yoga and yoga meditation, which I practised very diligently in every practical way within the constraints of my social obligations of education and family necessities.



Since I was 18, I have never had illness of any form except that which was self-inflicted. The experience also taught me that real learning comes from within.

Armed with a sound body, a stubborn mind and boundless energy I set out on a journey of this life that has been truly extraordinary but needless to say, meditation got a back seat. My interests in life include travel, people, writing, cooking, gardening, keeping fit, health, music (I play several instruments) and the esoteric.

By 22, I became a millionaire working on the copper mines in Northern Rhodesia during the day and playing in a band at night. I travelled around the world as a journalist, benchmarked the transition of Africa from a colonial continent to independence witnessing first-hand, wars, economic miracles and upheavals, the wonders of aid and assistance to those affected by drought, floods or the ravages of diseases; and mixed with presidents, paupers, musical icons, religious leaders and prostitutes.

In my personal life I have had the exceptional opportunity of many relationships – including three marriages – that has given me a broad insight into the interaction between people and how this interaction affects one's inner self. My three children, all from my first marriage, are now adults on their own journey through life in different parts of the world.



There is probably a book for each of the decades I have been on earth.

What is important is today. What is of critical importance is this moment. I justify this by asking: 'Have you ever been able to live except in this instant?'

So it is this moment in which I offer an explanation having taken you from where I have come and what I have done.

I have been on a journey of exploration. How fortunate that my cycle has taken me back to my 'inner being' as a 14-year-old. The rediscovery of this world – now with a different maturity – has changed even the colours all around me.

Through meditation I have been regenerated in mind, body and being. I see things and people as I have never seen them before. The scientific community has defined us as manifestations of vibrations. In fact all physical matter is no more than denser oscillations of cellular activity.

Around each of us is an energy field and beyond this, progressive scientific experiments tell us there may be countless more. Meditation enables me to associate more closely with these higher vibrations and bring about beneficial changes to my environment and myself.

The most important results are a great tolerance for everyone around me, protection for the environment through eliminating excess and wastage and the relief from stress, anxiety and anger encountered in everyday life.

Six months ago, I met Ron, the founder of the Peace for Africa Movement in South Africa. Through him and the monks now staying in this country, the importance of meditation was again awakened in me. Although I had read many books and studied related philosophies over the years, I still found it necessary to have guidance and support.



The essence of meditation is many people meditating together. It offers a truly cosmopolitan solution as when one closes one's eyes, there is no colour, creed or gender differences, or in fact for that matter, any cost.

It is a solution that I believe is the answer to the violence, anger and corruption in South Africa. In fact, it is truly amazing!

**Mr. Howard McCrary (U.S.A.)**



"After I learned about meditation, I think meditation allows us to know that, "You and I are one". The love from within fulfills us and makes us united. There is no "You" nor "I" but a "We" where we have each other. I believe that meditation will bring the ultimate world peace that everyone has been searching for."

My name is Howard McCrary and I am a jazz, hip hop, and gospel singer. I developed a single album called, "So Good", composed of religious songs. I have sung with, and compiled songs for many famous singers such as Michael Jackson and Chaka Kahn. Dubbing cartoons such as the California Raisins, I also chorused and appeared in a song in the Hollywood blockbuster, *Lady Killers* movie, and *Mighty Joe Young* movie.



When I was three years old, I began playing the piano without having had any prior lessons. At seven, a mysterious thing happened to me; I heard a voice whisper to me, "You'll be the instrument for World Peace." I doubted it and have been waiting for an answer for so long. I prayed for World Peace, but felt deeply inside that, "World Peace cannot arise until inner peace is found." Then I discovered inner peace during a meditation class at Wat Phra Dhammakaya. This has made me more confident and has given me a better understanding.

My first experience in meditation was what I never thought would be possible. Usually, it is dark when you close your eyes, isn't it? But I saw a light when I closed my eyes. The bright light inside filled me with happiness, peace, confidence, delight, and love, as if I received a magnificent power. I now feel kindness and compassion in my perceptions of people. I want to change my life so that it can change others as well.



I wish that everyone in the entire world would practice meditation because it is "the only thing that is truly useful". I like what Luang Phaw Dhammajayo once said, "Meditation is free", and it is so wonderful. Usually, what I have seen is that we have to pay for everything in this world, but we don't have to pay for meditation. It needs only time, attention, love, and the intention to make it happen. Each time while meditating, I see a light that becomes brighter and more concentrated like sunlight. It is the size of a small basketball. Then I see a bright and clear crystal ball at the center of my body. I feel a happiness that I never felt before in my life.



I believe meditation is not much different from playing the piano. When I first began playing the piano, I was not that good. I attentively and consistently practiced it every day. Now I am a professional composer, lead singer, chorus singer, and musician (piano and keyboard), and many people now say my skills are "legendary".

I have a dream of using my musical skills to create World Peace because songs are a universal language bringing people of different nationalities or religions into harmony. It is also easy to understand. I composed one song for the 1992 Winter Olympics, held in Germany recorded by Chaka Kahn & The Yellow Jackets, entitled, "You and I are one", to represent the unity and harmony of all countries. However, after I learned about meditation, I think meditation allows us to know that, "You and I are one". The love from within fulfills us and makes us united. There is no "You" nor "I" but a "We" where we have each other. I believe that meditation will bring the ultimate world peace that everyone has been searching for. I agree that if everyone learns to practice meditation, World Peace will happen. It is the day of celebration. I have dreamt of seeing World Peace since I was seven years old. I believe that the time is coming closer. We can see World Peace during our lifetime.

I won't stop meditating. I have never been happy and fulfilled like this before in my life. Now I can barely wait to meditate. I recently had a new inner experience when I began meditation by crossing my right leg over my left leg, thinking of the point where the breath ends, relaxing my body, and adjusting my mind so that it doesn't feel distressed, doubtful, greedy, expectant, hungry, angry, afraid, or covetous. All negative feelings before my closed eyes totally disappeared; only love and kindness remained. When I closed my eyes, unwavering for a moment, I saw the bright light of a crystal ball at the center of my body. I had never been happy like that before in my life. When I looked through the center of the crystal ball, I saw someone sitting in my abdomen. I saw only hands and shoulders at first. Observing him gently and with a still mind, I felt more familiar with him. It was getting slowly clearer that the person inside me was not a stranger. It was I, who was very bright like gold. My own astral body inside looked more handsome, more magnificent and younger than I. He was filled with peace and comfort. I felt like the passing of time had stopped from within. I very much wanted to stop time. It felt like I was meditating for just 10 minutes. But once I opened my eyes and looked at the clock, an hour had already passed! But I couldn't stop meditating.



What is important now is that my body and mind are so clean and clear because of abstaining from alcohol. I stopped drinking alcohol completely. I may work in a place that has consumers of alcoholic beverages, customers who enjoy buying me a drink because they like my music. Although I would not refuse it before, I now say, "No". They wonder and ask me why I won't drink. I tell them, "I can no longer drink because I am meditating. I cannot see inside with drunken eyes." They ask me with interest, "What is meditation"? I then say to them, "Would you like to know? I will tell you." I introduce meditation to them and tell them that no matter what their religion is, they can meditate. "Even though you are Christian, meditation will allow your Christian pathway to be more complete, wonderful and more beautiful. Disturbances will disappear. The more you meditate, the more your life will be continuously beautiful."



Meditation also improves my musical skills. When I play music, I have more alternative ways of playing. Now when I sing, I sing from my heart, from the source of light. I find myself gentler and have more goodwill towards people around me. I would like to tell everyone that there is a hope of World Peace. The important key is meditation, so anger and suffering can end. We have experienced war for so long. That is not an answer. Is it wrong to experience the meditation that Luang Phaw Dhammajayo teaches? One day I tried meditating, and meditation has changed my whole life, indeed. I think that once we all try meditating together, there will be one light and one peace. That day will be the day of World Peace without killing, greed, hostility, and war.

# PART 3

# Start Your Own Journey

*Chapter 8*

# Start Meditation Today

"The important point is to set aside time to meditate every day and make it a habit. You should do it regardless of whether you can meditate well or not. In order to obtain good results, you need to practise and accumulate "meditation time". It is like the pilot that needs to accumulate flight time until he can skillfully fly the airplane."

**Luang Phaw Dhammajayo**

## *The Universal Technique is to feel at ease and relaxed*

Meditation is not difficult. Just close your eyes and rest your focus at the centre of your stomach. Imagine that you are lying down on the grass and looking up at the stars at night. You feel relaxed and comfortable. But instead of looking at the sky, you are gazing upon a star in your body.

Close your eyes and clear the mind. You may visualise an apple, an orange or a grapefruit. You can visualise any neutral object as it will become clearer and evolve on its own accord. The technique is to visualise the object easily and gently. Just give it a try. Meditate as if you are resting. You have worked so hard all day long and it is time to take a break and give yourself a reward. Just still your mind and relax. Within a few minutes of finding your focus, something miraculous will happen. Find that innocent self that is still inside you. Meditate with an open mind.

When you meditate, you should feel comfortable. Banish all negative emotions. In your daily lives, to accomplish something, you have to pursue it with all your strength. You will be under pressure; you will need to think, analyse, criticise and follow certain procedures. In meditation, there is no need for that. Feel at ease. If you do it right, your body and mind shall be rewarded. Your body will become relaxed, expanding and disappearing into the atmosphere. It is a rewarding experience that encourages us to increasingly pursue meditation. You will have the desire to meditate and will feel that time goes by very quickly. Through this simple technique, one can attain inner happiness. You may think that it cannot possibly be this simple, but all you need to do is to meditate and relax. If you try to make it complicated and difficult, you will find yourself stressed and frustrated. Embrace the simple relaxed technique which can be used by people of all faiths, regardless of nationality or race to attain inner happiness.



When you attain universal happiness inside yourself, you will feel so overwhelmed with joy that you will not be able to adequately find words to describe it. No one can do this for you, you have to attain it yourself in order to understand how it feels like. It is like when you eat a chilli. Others may ask you how it tastes, but you can only tell them that it is spicy. They do not really know what spicy means until they try it for themselves.

Thus, one cannot describe inner happiness to others. You cannot attain inner peace for others and others cannot attain it for you. This is a truth of life. It must be done on your own.

The site for meditation can be at your home, at a meditation centre, or at any place that is quiet and calm. It should be well-ventilated and have just the right temperature, neither too hot nor too cold, so that you won't feel uncomfortable.



Finally, for the meditation posture, you should sit cross-legged. You can use a cushion or pillow to make your position more comfortable and help you to sit for a longer period. If you cannot sit cross-legged, you can sit on a chair or sofa or wherever you are comfortable and can sit for a long time. But you should not feel too comfortable because it can cause you to fall asleep.

## *Beginning the Journey to Inner Peace with Basic Dhammakaya Meditation*



Start by adjusting your sitting position. If you sit on the floor, sit cross-legged, right leg over the left leg, right hand over the left hand, palms up, your right index finger gently touching your left thumb. Place both hands on your lap comfortably, your head and back erect. If you feel uncomfortable in this position, you may sit on a chair or sofa. Adjust your position until you feel completely comfortable, so that the blood will circulate freely, and you breathe naturally.

Gently close your eyes comfortably, as if you were going to sleep. Do not squeeze your eyelids and do not shut them forcefully. Close them slightly. Do not close them tightly. Sit with a smile on your face. Next, take a deep breath. Inhale and exhale a few times. Breathe in deeply until you feel the air pass through your lungs and reach the middle of your abdomen, and slowly breathe out, through your nostrils. When you breathe in, imagine that each cell in your body is fully taking in the feeling of happiness and joyfulness, and when you breathe out, breathe out all your worries, and negative feelings. Take a moment to let go of all responsibilities relating to work, loved ones, family, study or anything else.

Let everything go. Let your mind be joyful, relaxed and free from all worry. Then, breathe normally. Relax every muscle in your body. Start to relax from the top of your head, down to your forehead. Relax the muscles in your face, eyelids, neck, and muscles in your shoulders, arms and down to the tips of your fingers. Relax the muscles of your back, your chest, your legs and all the way down to the tip of your toes. Let every part of your body relax. Don't let any part of your body contract, tighten or become tense.

Continue to relax until you feel that every part of your body and each cell in your body are completely relaxed. You are now in a state of complete relaxation whereby you can feel an emptiness, transparency and lightness. Now, make your mind joyful, cheerful, clear, pure and bright. Release and let go. Empty your mind.

Make your mind clear, pure and free from all thoughts. Imagine you are sitting alone in a vast, open space, full of freedom and peacefulness as if you never had any attachment in life, never had any problems and never knew anyone before.

Then, imagine that your body has no organs, assume it is a tube, a hole, a hollow vacuum like an inflated balloon or like a crystal or diamond cylinder, bright and clear. Let it be an open space, empty, hollow inside. You may feel your body get lighter and lighter, as if it is weightless; gradually melting away and becoming one with nature.



Let yourself enjoy this feeling of peacefulness. Now, bring your mind to focus to the centre of the body, in the middle of your abdomen, two fingers' width above the navel level. If you are a new practitioner, do not worry too much about the centre of the body's exact point; simply maintain your mind, softly and gently, in the middle of your abdomen. The way that you focus your mind at the centre of the body, is by comparing it to the lightness and gentleness of a bird's feather floating down from the sky and touching the calm surface of the water.

Imagine the soft touch of a bird's feather when it touches the surface of the water. Focus your mind at the centre of the body with this feeling. Maintain the feeling of relaxation in your body and mind continuously, while you focus your mind at the centre of the body in the middle of your abdomen. After you've found the starting point to focus your mind, softly imagine the meditation object within you, so that the mind can have something to focus on and not wander. You may imagine a shining sun, of any size that you like. It should be bright like the midday sun but clear and soothing as the moonlight on a fullmoon night.

To imagine this, you need to know the method. Slowly imagine with ease. Relax. Keep it simple, as you might think of a football, a car, a house, or anything that is familiar. Do not force your mind to think of the object to a point that it makes you feel tense. Do not use too much effort. Or else, you will stare at it and that is the wrong method. Gently imagine the object, and relax. It does not matter if it is not clear. Be satisfied with however clear it is. And maintain your mind calmly, let it stop and be still. Think of that shining sun continuously. Do not let your mind wander. If you do think of something else, maintain your mind by reciting the mantra.



Recite the mantra in your mind softly, as if the soft sounds were coming from the centre of the shining sun in the middle of your abdomen. Recite the mantra, "Samma Arahang… Samma Arahang… Samma Arahang…", which means: purify your mind, so that you will be free from the sufferings of life, or you can use any words,

# The Seven Bases of the Mind

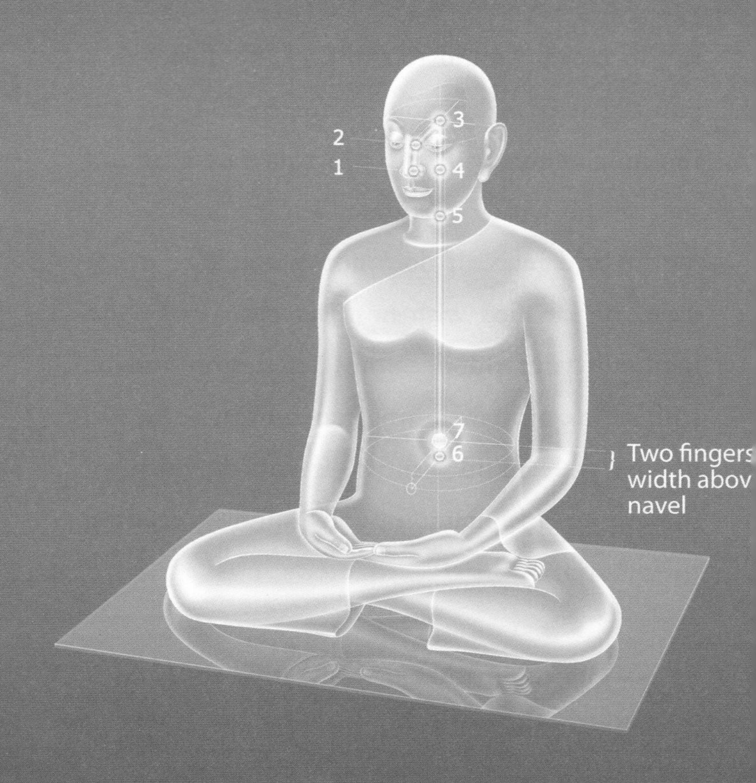


Base (1) Nostril { Left nostril for women / Right nostril for men

Base (2) Bridge of nose { Left for women / Right for men

Base (3) Middle part of head
Base (4) Roof of mouth
Base (5) Throat
Base (6) Navel
Base (7) Centre of gravity

# The Seven Bases of the Mind

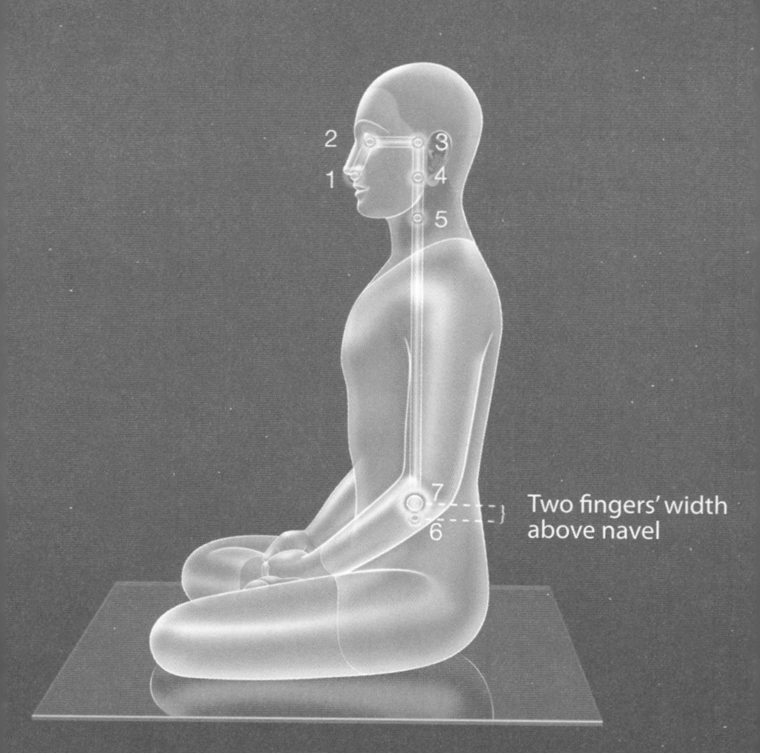


Base (1) Nostril { Left nostril for women / Right nostril for men

Base (2) Bridge of nose { Left for women / Right for men

Base (3) Middle part of head
Base (4) Roof of mouth
Base (5) Throat
Base (6) Navel
Base (7) Centre of gravity

such as "clear and bright, clear and bright, clear and bright". Recite the mantra continuously, whilst thinking of the bright sun, gently and comfortably. Focus your mind and be still at the centre of pure brightness. Maintain your mind by imagining a bright object and at the same time recite the mantra continuously, softly and comfortably until your mind is still.



Once your mind is completely still, it will drop the words, 'Samma Arahang' or "clear and bright" by itself, as if you are forgetting to recite this mantra, or feel that you don't want to recite the mantra anymore; or just want to be still, and the mind is not wandering or thinking about anything, and there is only the picture of the bright sun appearing clearly at the centre of the body. If you feel like this, you do not have to go back to reciting the mantra again. Let your awareness maintain the vision of the shining sun, gently and comfortably. Only do this from this point onward, with a still mind, softly, gently, constantly and continuously. Do not do anything beyond this.

If you have any experience from within which is different from your meditation object, do not be excited. Let your mind be neutral, as if you had a lot of previous experiences in life. Observe the experiences that occur with a calm mind and relax. Do not question how this happens. Just observe, otherwise your mind will move from the centre of the body and your inner experience will disappear. Observe it with a calm mind and be neutral, Soon, your mind will be completely focused, pure, still and feel nothingness. This moment is very important so do not neglect it, pay attention because the experience from within will progress and your mind should remain only in this state. Your role at this time is to be an observer. Just keep observing and just relax. Do not think of anything. Do all of this - only this, that is all.

If you do this correctly, easily and comfortably, then your mind will become still easily and effortlessly. If you were an analyst, you would analyse and comment on your inner experiences. Your mind would not be calm and all your good experience would go away. So, adhere only to these instructions. Eventually, your mind will be refined and completely focused at the centre of the body. The mind will deepen, entering into clarity, purity, brightness, true happiness and true inner knowledge, which is the wisdom that lies within. Finally, you will attain *Dhammakaya*, the inner self which is in you, that is universal, the same for everyone in this world.

# *Chapter 9*

# Meditation in Everyday Life

"As you meditate on a daily basis, you will notice the positive changes in your life, whether it is sleeping or waking up in peace, sitting, standing or walking with happiness. Your face will brighten and your skin will be rejuvenated. These features will attract others. Your speech will be powerful even though it is the same speech that you have had in the past. The difference is that your speech will now be voiced from a place of purity and fulfillment. This makes the speech pure, fulfilled and trustworthy altogether. The heart and the body will be filled with happiness."

**Luang Phaw Dhammajayo**

## *Happiness in every way*

As you meditate on a daily basis, you will notice the positive changes in your life, whether it is sleeping in peace or waking up in peace, sitting, standing or walking with happiness. Your face will brighten and your skin will be rejuvenated. These features will attract others. Your speech will be powerful even though it is the same speech that you have had in the past. The difference is that your speech will now be voiced from a place of purity and fulfillment. This makes the speech pure, fulfilled and trustworthy altogether. The heart and the body will be filled with happiness. Even if our surroundings are full of chaos, our minds will have found true happiness. It may be difficult to change our surroundings, so we have to adapt to it instead. We should elevate our minds above the surroundings to find true happiness. This is similar to a cool spot in the middle of a hot oven.

This is also a place where you feel as if you are sleeping in the midst of light. This is unlike the unconscious sleep whereby you are in darkness. You will fall asleep as you normally would, but after awhile, you will feel as if you are sleeping in the light. Once you wake up, you will wake up in light and be able to pull the happiness from the inside out. The inner happiness will slowly expand to the outside and bring happiness to a new day. From the time you take a shower, wash your face, brush your teeth and have your meal, to the time you go to work and school, the light of happiness will follow you wherever you go. Others will look up to you.

The happiness from meditation will spread to your surroundings and will rid your life of the bad, whether it is the weather, people, animals or material things. You have heard the testaments of people who speak of the inner happiness from having attained inner Dhamma. Hopefully, one of these days, you will attain the inner Dhamma and become the person who gives testaments to others in the world. On that day, you will be an important part of the effort to bring happiness to the world and be the source of motivation for others to live their lives in a positive way.



## *Daily activities and the mind should go together*

In order to achieve the benefits of meditation, you must practise meditation on a daily basis. You cannot miss even for a day. It should be done on a daily basis without excuses, even though you may be tired from work. You should set aside some time just for meditation in order to become familiar with the Middle Way. Business and the mind should go hand in hand. A business is used in the search for money to help nourish your life, and the mind is used to search for peace of mind in order to get rid of unhappiness.



Now that you know this, you must know how to manage your time. You should train your mind to be focused while you are sitting, sleeping, standing and walking. Try to settle your mind in the middle of your abdomen, in the middle way, by using either the shining sun or the clear crystal ball as an object of focus. Do this on a daily basis and make it a habit just like when you wake up in the morning. You take a shower, wash your face, brush your teeth, and perform your daily activities without someone having to remind you. We do these things on a daily basis not because someone compels us to, but rather because they are necessities in life. This is in the same way that meditation is a necessity for your mind. You automatically perform activities that are important for your body on a daily basis. Likewise, you should be doing what is important for your mind on a daily basis as well. The more you practise, the better you will be, and it will become second nature to you. This is similar to when you breathe while eating, scratching while moving your leg or watching while listening.



Therefore, moving and being still can go together. Your career and your mind must work together. Internal and external life of the body should be allocated 50 percent each. A balanced and complete life should add up to 100 percent. If you can lead your life like this, then your life will be complete. You can work while your mind is still; and you can talk, look or listen while your mind is still.

You should train your mind to be still even though you were not trained to do so since childhood. Instead, you were trained to not be still, to always think and search for people, animals or things. It may be difficult at first to be still, since you are so used to not being still. However, you should not give up. Keep practising every day and night and incorporate it into every activity that you do whether it is working for a living, studying or taking care of your family.

# *The Ten Homework Assignments for Meditation Practitioners*

To improve our meditation experience, we must always observe how well we meditate every day. We should figure out the cause of poor or good meditation experiences each day. For example, some days you might be able to still your mind very well because you had a good rest the night before, or you feel refreshed due to a short exercise in the evening. On other days, you may feel tense and have a poor meditation experience because of stress from work. We should observe how daily activities affect meditation experiences, which will allow us to correct the causes of poor meditation and get involved in activities resulting in good meditation.

I would like to suggest some guidelines which should be followed in conjunction with your daily activities, from the time you wake up till the time you go to sleep. The guidelines are called, *The Ten Homework Assignments for Meditation Practitioners*. These guidelines, when followed, generate a refreshing and relaxing feeling all day long. Additionally, when it is time for us to meditate, our minds will be able to readily come to a standstill.



The Ten Homework Assignments are:

1. Upon waking up, immediately reconnect your attention with the centre of the body.

2. Before getting up, take a minute to recollect that you are lucky to be alive

and remind yourself that you will surely die one day in future. Spread love and kindness to all living beings in the world.

3. Throughout the day, create the feeling that you are united with the meditation object at the centre of the body.



4. Take one minute of every hour to still your mind and think of the meditation object at the centre of the body.

5. Recollect the meditation object at the centre of the body while conducting other activities throughout the day.

6. Make the world a nicer place to live in by smiling and speaking in an endearing way.

7. Make the effort to see the virtues in yourself and others. Congratulate others on their virtues and give them the opportunity to congratulate yours.

8. Keep daily notes of your meditation experiences in a diary.



9. Before going to sleep, recollect the good deeds you have done throughout the day.

10. Centre your mind before falling asleep.

**The Ten Homework Assignments can be summarized into three groups based on their benefits. The first group aims at helping us to position our minds at the middle of our bodies.** (Assignments #1, 3, 4, 5 and 10). Irrespective of our daily activities, we should regularly position our minds centrally at the middle of the body, which is 2 finger-widths above our navel level. Accustom our minds to the meditation object which could be either a crystal sphere, a diamond, the sun, moon or stars.

When we are not meditating, we should still imagine the meditation object in a relaxed manner without coercion. Keep at it without any expectations; it doesn't matter if the meditation object appears clearly in your mind or not. The purpose is to accustom your mind to remain at the body's centre. Subsequently, when we close our eyes for meditation, we will be able to position our minds easily. If we could do this all day, our minds would readily be at the centre each time we close our eyes. Our minds would become still easily, softly and gently.

**The second group aims at focusing our mind on positive things or virtues that refresh our mind** (Assignments #2, 6, 7 and 9). Good virtues include loving kindness towards all beings - a smiling and cheerful manner, positive speech, the ability to see good virtues in others and ourselves, rejoicing in others' and our own virtues as well as the recollection of our virtues each day. By accustoming our mind to these virtues, our minds will be clear and illuminated and we won't be easily irritated. Subsequently, we will be able to still our mind easily when we meditate.



**The third group focuses on keeping a record of meditation experiences** (Assignment #8). This record keeping helps us track the cause of a satisfying or unsatisfying experience during meditation. You should keep a meditation diary on days that you meditate well as well as days that you don't. Keep a diary and take notice of how your meditation experience improves. Use a meditation diary as your meditation master.

## *Sharing loving kindness*

The sharing of loving kindness is something we can do everyday, both before and after daily meditation. A brief period of sharing loving kindness before meditating, softens and broadens our minds. The sharing of loving kindness as such helps improve our meditation experience.



A brief session of sharing loving kindness after meditation spreads the purity of our meditated minds around ourselves first, and subsequently towards others. The benefits of sharing loving kindness everyday include radiating a happy feeling when we are awake and asleep. If we have dreams, they will be sweet and auspicious. We will be rid of anger and we will be positive thinkers. Most importantly, it will greatly help to improve our meditation. We can share loving kindness simply by doing the following:

Before ending our meditation session and when our minds come to a standstill and hence filled with happiness, we can actually share loving kindness, good wishes and peacefulness with all other people in the world. We can start by focusing our stilled mind at the centre of our body where we feel true love and good wishes towards all beings. Let all good feelings coalesce into a bright crystal sphere filled with love and good wishes. Without any effort, imagine the crystal sphere of love and good wishes expanding in all directions from the body's centre towards all other beings.

Wish everyone freedom from suffering, and ultimately help them attain extreme happiness from meditation. Meditation brings our mind back to its original pure state. Furnish them with the ability to incorporate attained happiness to enrich their perfect and virtuous daily lives. The lives they lead will therefore prove beneficial for themselves and others.



Feel the expansion of our bright spherical minds all around ourselves and towards people in our surroundings regardless of whether they are near or far. Expand our minds to cover our site for meditation and continually outwards until it covers the whole sky. Feel unlimited love and kindness towards people of the world in every continent and elsewhere, irrespective of their nationalities, religions and ethnicities.

Let our minds connect with all others. Wish them happiness, wish every country prosperity and hope that the world will be filled with only good people who bring true peace and happiness to humankind. Let the purity of our still minds expand from the centre towards other people of the world who are suffering as a result of war, to attain true peace. Wish that everyone will stop taking advantage of one another and are determined to turn the dark side of their minds into kind and loving minds.



The purity of our minds during meditation radiate outwards as a mass of purity, silently into the atmosphere. The purity cleanses defilements and darkness from our own minds and others. Their minds and our minds become bright and clear, hence we can now lead our lives in the right direction - a direction towards happiness and virtue. Eventually, we will change the world and bring true peace to the world.

## *The Next Step for Meditation Practitioners*

There are some drawbacks when practising the *Dhammakaya* meditation technique, by consulting this meditation manual exclusively without a meditation master. Each individual practitioner has a different personality which results in different difficulties during meditation. The manual can solve some basic questions but not all. Many new practitioners have questions that may make their meditation practices progress slowly, if not halt it completely.

As a suggestion, I would like to invite all those who have tried practising meditation after reading this book to come to Wat Phra Dhammakaya or any of its branches worldwide. There, you will have a chance to speak with meditation instructors who can provide good suggestions for better meditation and answer unresolved questions about meditation. Visiting Wat Phra Dhammakaya or its branches will introduce you to other practitioners with similar interests. The group study and meditation session provides group support and encouragement towards improving your meditation. If you wish to advance in meditation practice, you can participate in the seven-day meditation retreat for foreigners. The temple offers monthly meditation retreats in Thailand. (www.meditationthai.org)

# *Appendix*

# About the Author

## Luang Phaw Dhammajayo



Luang Phaw Dhammajayo (The Most Venerable Dhammajayo Bhikkhu) was born in Singburi Province, Central Thailand, on April 22, 1944. His interest in Buddhism began in his childhood, when he embarked in Dhamma study and continuous meditation practice, and especially so when he met The Master Nun Chand Khonnokyoong (Khun Yay Ajahn). She was an advanced Dhammakaya Meditation practitioner and instructor who was one of the forefront disciples of The Great Master Phramongkolthepmuni (Luang Pu Wat Paknam), the past famous abbot of Wat Paknam Bhasicharoen who discovered the Dhammakaya Meditation technique. The Master Nun taught Luang Phaw Dhammajayo all that she knew about the Dhammakaya Meditation which she had learned from The Great Master.



When Luang Phaw Dhammajayo later graduated from Kasetsart University in Bangkok, he was ordained to the order of Buddhist monks at Wat Paknam Bhasicharoen in 1969 by his preceptor, His Holiness Somdet Phra Maharatchamongkhalachan, the present abbot of Wat Paknam Bhasicharoen. Upon his ordination into the Buddhist monk order, he was given the name "Dhammajayo" which means "The Victory through Dhamma".

In the following years, The Master Nun and Luang Phaw Dhammajayo, along with their close devotees, established a new site for meditation practice in the Khlong Sam sub-district, Khlong Luang district, Pathum Thani province, Thailand, which has been developed into the beautiful and clean Wat Phra Dhammakaya where thousands of monks, novice monks and laymen reside. There are also tens of thousands of people who join the Buddhist ceremonies and meditation practice at the temple on a regular basis.



Luang Phaw Dhammajayo has dedicated himself to meditation practice and instructions, Dhamma study, and the promotion of world peace through inner peace, especially for the attainment of the *Dhammakaya* - which he has said is the true nature that everyone can attain within, regardless of race, religion, gender, age and belief.

Presently, Luang Phaw Dhammajayo is the abbot of Wat Phra Dhammakaya and president of the Dhammakaya Foundation, which has many branches both in Thailand and abroad. The foundation is very active in promoting peace, meditation practice, Dhamma study and in providing assistance to society. In addition, he also hosts the "Inner Dreams Kindergarten Programme" via the DMC channel which is broadcast daily worldwide via satellites and the internet (www.dmc.tv/en). The programme is rich in Buddhist philosophy and is aimed at providing knowledge, understanding the truth about life concerning all beings in a modern and interesting context, meditation guidance and providing enjoyment for viewers at the same time.

# *Dhammakaya Meditation Societies Worldwide*

## Wat Phra Dhammakaya

23/2 Mu 7, Khlong Sam, Khlong Luang
Pathum Thani 12120, Thailand
Tel: +(66-2) 831-1000
+(66-2) 524-0257 to 63
Fax: +(66-2) 524-0270 to 1
Email: info@dhammakaya.or.th
www.dhammakaya.or.th
www.meditationthai.org
www.dmc.tv/en

# ASIA

## BRUNEI

*Co-ordination Office*

Contact: Ruangrassame Chareonying
Tel: +(673) 8-867-029
Email: JY_dhamma@yahoo.com
Thailand Co-ordinator contact:
Ms. Rawiwon Mechang
Tel: +(66)-5-071-0190

## CHINA

### Sichuan

*Sichuan Meditation Center*

Tel: +(86) 28-8541-8878
+(86) 28-8129-2072
Mobile: +(86) 136-8900-7101
Email: nui072@hotmail.com
pp072@yahoo.com

## HONG KONG

*The Dhammakaya International Society of Hong Kong Ltd.*

385-391, 2/F, Henning House, Hennessy Rd,
Wanchai, Hong Kong
Tel: +(852) 2762-7942
+(852) 2794-7485
Fax:+(852) 2573-2800
Email: dmchk@netvigator.com

# JAPAN

## Ibaraki

*Wat Bhavana Ibaraki*
2816-2 Oaza Arakawahongo, Ami-Machi,
Inashiki-gun, Ibaraki-ken, Japan 300-1152
Tel: +(81) 2-9846-6110
Mobile: +(81) 080-5489-5669
+(81) 080-5489-6659
Email: Ibaraki_otera@msn.com

## Kanagawa

*Wat Bhavana Kanagawa*
243-4006 Kanagawaken, Ebinashi,
kokubukita, 3-39-9, Japan
Tel: +(81) 4-6205-6713
Fax: +(81) 4-6205-6714
Mobile: +(81) 80-5099-4527
+(81) 80-3458-6028
Email: puwanat072@hotmail.com

## Nagano

*Wat Thai Nagano*
733-3 Mihari, Tomi-Shi, Nagano-Ken,
389-0501, Japan
Tel: +(81) 2-6864-7516
+(81) 2-6864-7720
Fax: +(81) 2-6862-2505
Mobile: +(81) 90-9390-6055
Email: yanakuno@yahoo.com

## Osaka

***Wat Bhavana Osaka***

Dhammakaya International Meditation Center of Osaka
(DIMC of Osaka)
4-6-27 Ohmiya, Asahi-ku, Osaka,
535-0002, Japan
Tel: +(81) 6-6956-1400
Fax: +(81) 6-6956-1401
Email: dimcosaka@hotmail.com



## Tochigi

***Wat Bhavana Tochigi***

1068 Oya-Machi, Utsunomiya-shi,
Tochigi-ken, Japan 321-0345
Tel: +(81) 2-8652-8701 to 2
+(81) 2-8652-8703
Email: krubajane39@hotmail.com

## Tokyo

***Dhammakaya International Meditation Center of Tokyo***

3-78-5 Arakawa, Arakawa-ku, Tokyo,
116-0002, Japan
Tel: +(81) 3-5604-3021
Fax: +(81) 3-5604-3022
Email: chalapinyo@yahoo.com

# MALAYSIA

## Kuala Lumpur

*Persatuan Meditasi Dhammakaya Selangor (Dhammakaya Meditation Association,Selangor)*

4-2, Jalan Puteri 5/1, Bandar Puteri,
47100 Puchong, Selangor D.E., Malaysia
Tel: +(60) 3-8063-1882
Mobile: +(60) 17-331-1599
Email: chutintharo072@hotmail.com



## Penang

*Dhammakaya Meditation Center of Penang*

66, Lengkonk Kenari1, Sungai Ara,
11900 Penang, Malaysia
Tel: +(60) 4-644-1854
Fax: +(60) 19-457-4270 to 1
Email: dmcpn@hotmail.com

# SINGAPORE

*Kalyanamitta Centre (Singapore)*

30 Mohamed Sultan Road
#03-03 Lam Ann Building, Singapore 238974
Tel: +(65) 6836-1620
Email: dimcsg@dhammakaya.or.th
dimcsg@singnet.com.sg

## SOUTH KOREA

*Wat Tae Jong Sa*
M 29-4, Dongsam-2 dong, Youndo-Gu,
Busan City, Republic of Korea
Tel:+(82) 51-405-2626
Mobile: +(82) 10-8681-5976
+(82) 10-2996-9072

## TAIWAN R.O.C.

### Taipei



***Dhammakaya International Meditation Center of Taipei***
3F No.9 Lane 16, Sec.2 Sihchuan Rd.,
Banciao city, Taipei country 220
Tel: +(886) 2-8966-1000
Fax: +(886) 2-8967-2800
http://dhammakaya.tc

### Taizhong

***Dhammakaya International Meditation Center of Taizhong***
1-2F, No. 25, Lane 14, Minquan Rd., Zhong Dis,
Taizhong City
Tel: +(886) 4-2223-7663

### Taoyuan

***Dhammakaya International Meditation Center of Taoyuan***
No. 232, Ching-Tian Street, Taoyuan City 330
Tel: +(886) 3-377-1261
Mobile: +(886) 9-2252-1072
Email: watthaitaoyuan@hotmail.com

# The Middle East

## BAHRAIN

***DMC Centre, Bahrain***

1310 Road No. 5641, Block No.0356,
Manama City, Bahrain
Contact: Mr.Thanachai & Mrs.Peanjai Thongthae
Tel: +(973) 3960-7936
Email: s4p04u@hotmail.com

## IRAN

***Co-ordination Office***

Contact: Ms. Aroona Puenebue
Tel: +(98) 21-2260-2105
Email: marissa_ange@yahoo.com

## OMAN

***Co-ordination Office***

Contact: Ms. Rathanavadee Boonprasert
Tel: +(968) 9901-4584

## QATAR

***Co-ordination Office***

Contact: Ms. Naviya Tonboonrithi
Tel: +(974) 572-7178
Email: naviyatonboonrithi@yahoo.com

## SAUDI ARABIA

***Co-ordination Office***

Contact: Mr. Udom Chimnuan
Tel: +(966) 50-899-1912
Email: saudom_80@yahoo.com

## DUBAI

***Co-ordination Office***

P.O.Box 33084, Dubai, UAE.
Contact:
Ms. Sangmanee Tel: +(971) 50-770-4508
Mr. Methin Tel: +(971) 50-754-0825
Ms. Dussadee Tel: +(971) 50-228-5077

## The Middle East

***Thailand Co-ordinator***

Contact: Ms. Rawiwon Mechang
Tel: +(668)-5-071-0190
Email: rawi0072@yahoo.com

# Africa

## SOUTH AFRICA

### Cape Town

***Cape Town Meditation Centre (CMC.)***

4B Homlfirth Road, Sea Point, Cape Town,
South Africa, 8005
Tel: +(27) 21-439-1896
Mobile: +(27) 72-323-0060
+(27) 79-379-0245

### Johannesburg

***Johannesburg Meditation Centre***

30 Scheepers Street, North Riding,
Randburg, Johannesburg, South Africa 2169
Tel: +(27) 11-704-3360
Mobile: +(27) 72-363-1226
+(27) 78-464-8871
Email: info@watthaiafrica.org
somsaknow@gmail.com

# Europe

## BELGIUM

### Antwerp

***Dhammakaya International Meditation Centre (Belgium)***

Sint-Jobsteenweg 84, 2970 'S-Gravenwezel,
Antwerp, Belgium
Tel: +(32) 3.326.45.77,
+(32) 3.289.51.81
Mobile: +(32) 494.32.60.02
Email: ppujakaro@hotmail.com

## DENMARK

### Copenhagen

***Wat Buddha Denmark***

Gl.Landevej 12,7130 Juelsminde, Denmark
Tel: +(45) 46.59.00.72
Mobile: +(45) 20.70.74.59
Email: dimc_dk@yahoo.com

## FRANCE

### Bordeaux

***Wat Bouddha Bordeaux***

47, Cours du General de Gaulle,
33170 Gradignan, France
Tel: +(33) 5.40.00.93.70
Mobile: +(33) 6.20.23.53.08
Email: wat_bdx@hotmail.com

**Paris**

***Wat Bouddha Paris***

10, Avenue de Paris, 77164 Ferrieres en Brie, France
Tel: +(33) 1.64.77.28.37
Fax: +(33) 6.88.25.82.06
Email: vichak@yahoo.com

**Strasbourg**

***Dhammakaya Centre International de la Meditation***

21, Boulevard de Nancy, 67000 Strasbourg, France
Tel: +(33) 3.88.32.69.15
Fax: +(33) 3.88.22.99.19
Email: dimcfr@yahoo.com

## GERMANY

**Koenigsbrunn**

***Dhammakaya International Meditation Zentrum (DIMZ)***

Heinkel Str. 1,86343 Koenigsbrunn, Germany
Tel: +(49) 8231.957.4530
Fax: +(49) 8231.957.4532
Mobile: +(49) 162.421.0410
Email: ppadec@hotmail.com

### Frankfurt

***Wat Buddha Frankfurt***

***(Meditation Verein Frankfurt Me.V)***

Odenwald Str.22, 65479, Ruanheim, Germany
Tel: +(49) 614.2833.0888
Fax: +(49) 614.2833.0890
Email: lpjon2499@hotmail.com

### Stuttgart

***Wat Buddha Stuttgart***



Im Meissel Str.6, 71111, Waldenbuch, Germany
Tel: +(49) 715.753.8187
Fax: +(49) 715.753.7677
Mobile: +(49) 16.0179.3782
Email: wat_stuttgart@hotmail.com

### Bodensee

***Wat Buddha Bodensee***

Lindauer Str. 76, 88085 Langenargen, Germany
Tel: +(49) 754.393.9777
Email: Wat_Bodensee@hotmail.com

## ITALY

### Milan

***Wat Buddha Milano***

Via Dello Scoiattolo 7 21052
Busto Arsizio (VA) Italy
Tel: +(39) 33.138.6721
+(39) 33.131.8738
Email: fortunebigbank@msn.com,
janda.a@hotmail.it

## NORWAY

### Midnattsol

***Wat Buddha Midnattsol***

***(Det Norske Dhammakaya Samfunn)***

Hvittingfossveien 343,
3080 Holmestrand Norway
Tel: +(47) 33.61.01.43
Mobile: +(47) 997.23.075
Fax: +(47) 33.09.66.09
Email: dhammakaya-norway@hotmail.com
http://www.dhammakaya.no

## SWEDEN

### Hisings Backa

***Wat Buddha Gothenburg***

Ostra Arodsgatan 17B, 422 43,
Hisings Backa, Sweden
Tel: +(46) -31.58.57.99
Mobile: +(46) -737.562.722
Fax: +(46) 8668-8993
Email: pworalert@hotmail.com

## SWITZERLAND

### Geneva

***Wat Buddha Geneva, Switzerland***

Avenue d'aire 93 G, 1203 Geneva, Switzerland
( c/o Wee Khee Wee )
Tel: +(41) 796.049.704
Mobile: +(33) 06.15.41.70.14

# THE UNITED KINGDOM

## Bristol

*Wat Buddha Bristol*
7 Grange Close, Bradley Stoke,
Bristol, BS32 OAH, United Kingdom
Tel: +(44) 1454-617434
Mobile: +(44) 7723-351254
Email: virandharo@hotmail.com

## London



*Wat Phra Dhammakaya London*
(Dhammakaya International Society of
United Kingdom)
2 Brushfield Way, Knaphill, Woking,
GU21 2TG, UK
Tel: +(44) 1483-475757
+(44) 1483-480001
Fax: +(44) 1483-476161
Email: disuk@hotmail.co.uk

## Manchester

*Wat Charoenbhavana Manchester*
Gardner House, Cheltenham Street, Salford,
Manchester M6 6WY, United Kingdom
Tel: +(44) 161-736—1633
+(44) 798-882-3616
Fax: +(44) 161-736—5747
Email: watmanchester@hotmail.com

# North America

## THE UNITED STATES OF AMERICA

### California

*Dhammakaya International Meditation Center (USA)*

801 E. Foothill Blvd., Azusa, CA 91702 USA
Tel: +(1)-626-334-2160
Fax: +(1)-626-334-0702
Email: dimcazusa@yahoo.com
http://www.dimc.net



### Florida

*Florida Meditation Center*

1303 N. Gordon St., Plant City, FL 33563 USA
Tel: +(1)-813-719-8000
+(1)-813-719-8005
Fax: +(1)-813-719-8007
Email: pamotito@msn.com

### Georgia

*Georgia Meditation Center Inc.*

4522 Tilly Mill Road, Atlanta, GA 30360 USA
Tel: +(1)-770-452-1111
+(1)-770-643-1233
Mobile: +(1)-404-514-7721
+(1)-404-862-7559
Fax: (1)-770-452-3424
Email: somboonusa@yahoo.com

## Hawaii

***Hawaii Meditation Center***

54-111 Maakua Rd., Hauula, HI 97617 USA
Tel: +(1)-808-497-4072
Email: saiwa072@hotmail.com

## Illinois

***Meditation Center of Chicago (M.C.C.)***

6224 W.Gunnison St., Chicago, IL 60630 USA
Tel: +(1)-773-763-8763
Fax: +(1)-773-763-7897
Email: mcc_072@yahoo.com

## Minnesota

***Minnesota Meditation Center***

242 Northdale Blvd NW, Coon Rapids,
MN 55448 USA
Tel: +(1)-763-862-6122
Fax: +(1)-763-862-6123
Email: MMC_072@yahoo.com
psuriya@hotmail.com

## New Jersey

***Dhammakaya International Meditation Center of New Jersey***

257 Midway Ave., Fanwood, NJ 07023 USA
Tel: +(1)-908-322-4187
+(1)-908-322-4032
Fax: +(1)-908-322-1397
Email: dimc_nj@yahoo.com

## Oregon

***Oregon Meditation Center***

13208 SE. Stark Street., Portland,
OR 97233 USA
Tel: +(1)-503-252-3637
Mobile:+(1)-503-799-8547
Email: omc072@yahoo.com
http://www.dimcor.org

## Texas

***Meditation Center of Texas***

1011 Thannisch Dr., Arlington, TX 76011 USA
Tel: +(1)-817-275-7700
Email: meditation.ct.tx@gmail.com

## Washington

***Seattle Meditation Center***

852 N.E. 83rd Street Seattle, WA 98115 USA
Tel: +(1)-206-522-1514
Fax: +(1)-206-985-2920
Email: pmsamma@hotmail.com
phracheep@yahoo.com

## Virginia

***Meditation Center of D.C.***

3325 Franconia Rd., Alexandria, VA 22310 USA
Tel: +(1)-703-329-0350
Fax:+(1)-703-329-0062
Email: mdc072@yahoo.com

# CANADA

## Ottawa

*Co-ordination Office*

354 Breckenridge Cres.Ottawa,
Ontario K2W1J4, Canada
Contact: Pattrawan Sukantha
Tel: 613-254-9809
613-261-4341
Email: jayy.dee@hotmail.com

## Montreal

*Co-ordination Office*

3431 Jeanne-Manae Suite #8,
Quebec H2x2J7, Canada
Contact: Gritsana Sujjinanont
Tel: 514-845-5002
514-726-1639
Email: gritsana@netzero.net

## Toronto

Contact: Pipat Sripimolphan
Tel: 647-886-0347
Email: psripimolphan@yahoo.com

# Oceania

## AUSTRALIA

### Sydney Retreat

***Wat Phra Dhammakaya, Sydney***

Lot 3, Inspiration Place, Berrilee, NSW 2159
Tel: +(61) 2-9655-1128
Fax: +(61) 2-9655-1129
Mobile: +(61) 4-1162-8677
Email: Satit@dhammakaya.org.au

### Sydney Office

***Sydney Meditation Centre***

117 Homebush Rd. Strathfield NSW 2135, Australia
Tel: +(61) 2-9742-3031
Fax: +(61) 2-9742-3431
Mobile: +(61) 4-1145-3946
http://www.dhammakaya.org.au
http://www.dmctv.net.au

### Brisbane

***Brisbane Meditation Centre***

73 Lodge Rd., Wooloowin, Brisbane, QLD 4030, Australia
Tel: +(61) 7-3857-3431
Mobile: +(61) 4-3105-7215
Email: kentibkaeo@yahoo.com

## Melbourne

***Dhammakaya Meditation Centre of Melbourne***

84 Oakwood Rd., St. Albans VIC 3021, Australia
Tel: +(61) 3-9266-0181
Mobile: +(61) 4-0100-8799
Email: ronrawee@yahoo.com.au

## Perth

***Dhammakaya Meditation Centre of Perth***

174 Moolanda Boulevard, Kingsley,
WA, 6026, Australia
Tel: +(61) 8-9409-8614
Fax: +(61) 8-9408-1007
Mobile: +(61) 4-302-07877
Email: phra_tawee@yahoo.com.au

## Northern Beach

***Northern Beach Meditation Centre***

4 Hurdis Avenue, Frenchs Forest,
Sydney, Australia
Tel: +(61) 294511-722

# NEW ZEALAND

## Orewa

***Orewa Meditation Centre***

43 Albatross Road, Red Beach, HBC,
Auckland, New Zealand, 1461
Tel: +(64) 9-427-4263
Fax: +(64) 9-427-4264
Mobile: +(64) 21-153-8592
Email: orewameditation@yahoo.com.au

## Dunedin

***Dunedin Meditation Centre (DDMC)***

10 Barnes Drive, Caversham, Dunedin,
New Zealand, 9001
Tel: +(64) 3-487-6772
Fax: +(64) 3-487-6775
Email: thep072@yahoo.com

## SOLOMON ISLANDS

***Co-ordination Office***

KITANO WKK JV P.O.BOX 1108
Honiara Solomon Islands
Contact: Mr. Sangwian Khanchaiyaphum
Tel: +(677) 24808
Fax: +(677) 25460
Email: peleyo3@hotmail.com

# Credits

## Honorary Consultant:

Phrabhavanaviriyakhun
(Most Ven. Dattajeevo Bhikkhu)

## Consultants:

Ven. Somchai Thanavuddho (Ph.D)
Ven. Paladsudham Sudhammo
Ven. Bundit Varapanyo
Ven. Wissanu Penyateepo
Ven. Amnuaysak Munisakko
Ven. Nicholas Thanissaro
Ven. Sanchaya Nakajayo
Ven. Ronnapob Jotilabho
Voravudh Vorasubin
Vanna Chirakiti
Virongrong Ratanachaya
Metta Suvachitvong
Apichart Chivatxaranukul

**Translators:**

Aaron Stern (Ph.D)
Anchalee Stern
Jatuporn Kamphonphanitwong
Jarin Kamphonphanitwong
Kingkarn Rangsimonkamol
Naruemol Kamphonphanitwong
Niramon Kuyakanon
Nithivadee Tantipoj
Panadda Thanasuansan
Shinavit Sukhawat
Suganda Cluver
Suphichaya Panprasert (Ph.D)
Suradee Burnett
Therapong Chirasuphakorn
Tippawan Aramphongphun
Walairat Bumrongjaroen (Ph.D)
Witinya Kamphonphanitwong
Wiwat Kamolpornwijit (Ph.D)

**Art Direction & Design:**

Metta Suvachitvong and DM&S Advertising Co., Ltd.
The Print Lodge Pte. Ltd.

The Publisher would also like to extend appreciation to all individuals who have contributed in one way or another towards the success of this book.

# Tomorrow The World Will Change

Luang Phaw Dhammajayo

"The dream of world peace will never come true if the dreamer is unable to find his or her own inner contentment. Once everyone experience inner happiness, true world peace will occur."

What would a world of peace be like?

In the light of never-ending conflicts, wars and terrorist threats, peace is something that seems unattainable. Constantly wrought with uncertainty and hostility, life on this planet sometimes does seem lacklustre and lacking in joy; much less peaceful.

While most of us would think that the dream of world peace coming true is akin to catching the wind with our bare hands, Luang Phaw Dhammajayo, abbot of Dhammakaya Temple and president of Dhammakaya Foundation, brings an encouraging message: that world peace is within reach ... and all it takes is a simple practice.

Through the act of meditation – stilling the mind and focusing the mind at the centre of the body – every individual, regardless of race, culture and religion, can experience inner happiness that will ultimately perpetuate goodness and harmony on earth. Innate happiness, through meditation, has the power to purge inner demons such as greed and anger – the root cause of strife on earth – from the hearts of humanity.

Discover how you, as an individual, can gain a deeper understanding of life to combat the negativities of this world by first reaching an inner calm. *Tomorrow The World Will Change* not only gives you an overview on how meditation can make you a better person; it teaches you how to master meditation through its step-by-step meditation guide.

ISBN: 978-981-05-7757-5 (Singapore)
96 pages • 105mm (W) x 170mm (H)

# Journey to Joy

Luang Phaw Dhammajayo

Life is not merely an external voyage to achieve our goals; it is a journey whereby we look into ourselves and embark on the path to self-discovery for the attainment of Dhammakaya — the true refuge within everyone.

Within the pages of this book, Luang Phaw Dhammajayo shares how meditation plays a part in enriching peoples' lives. Meditation brings about bountiful love, instils hope and willpower, develops closer family relationships, increases a person's knowledge, enhances peoples' careers and leads them to unearth their inner wisdom and their ability to create everlasting peace.

To meditate, simply close your eyes, concentrate on the stillness and rest your focus at the seventh base of your body, two fingers' width above the navel. Experience absolute serenity and bliss by relaxing your mind and body in the process.

Your future lies in your hands. The journey towards ultimate happiness begins with you. Start meditation today and witness the positive changes in your life unfold before you!

ISBN: 978-981-05-9637-8 (Singapore)
368 pages • 110mm (W) x 178mm (H)

# Lovely Love

Luang Phaw Dhammajayo

Love, like all things in life, can be transient. Pure love, however, is lasting and it gives without necessarily bargaining for a return.

Within the pages of this book, Luang Phaw Dhammajayo teaches us how to love unselfishly by advocating that it does not matter whom you love, or how you love, but that you just love. A superior love that supersedes all others is universal love – a love which is pure, clean, complete and powerful. The best news is universal love can be attained simply through meditation. Meditating allows your mind to experience peace, pure happiness and pure love.

Reveal in the fact that the sole happiness in life is to love and be loved. Speak lovingly, think lovingly and act lovingly towards others and experience the infinite joy that pure love will bring into your life consequentially!

ISBN: 978-981-08-0044-4 (Singapore)
188 pages • 110mm (W) x 178mm (H)

The following book are available by mail-order:

**Tomorrow The World Will Change**

US$9.95

---

**Journey to Joy**

US$18.00/book
US$180.00/series [10 books]

---

**Lovely Love**

US$14.00/book
US$84.00/series [6 books]

---

Prices exclude postage and packing

Please send your enquiries or orders to:

# *Note*

# *Note*

# *Note*

# *Note*

# *Note*